SLAVERY EXAMINED

IN THE

LIGHT OF THE BIBLE.

BY LUTHER LEE.

SYRACUSE, N. Y.:
WESLEYAN METHODIST BOOK ROOM,
60 South Salina Street.

———

1855.

Republished by
Negro History Press – P. O. Box 5129 – Detroit, Michigan 48236

113445

Library of Congress Catalog Card Number: 76-92434
ISBN 0-403-00166-8

PREFACE.

*541
Lee*

The subject discussed in the following pages has occupied a large share of public attention for the last twenty years. This attention has been deepening, and becoming more general, and is still progressing, and the writer believes it will advance until the eye of the nation will be fixed upon the great subject of human rights. Slavery is so great and glaring a wrong, as to be able to live, only by diverting attention, or by perverting the Scriptures, conscience, and common sense. Let the eye of the nation become fixed on the system of American Slavery, and let its merits be freely examined in the light of the Scriptures, and let the sacred volume be disabused of the pro-slavery glasses which have blurred its pages, that its true light may be evolved, and Slavery will die for want of moral darkness, the only element in which it can live.

With all honest believers in the Christian Religion, the Scriptures are the "higher law," the only authoritative standard of right and wrong, and with them a successful appeal to the Bible is conclusive, the end of all controversy. Such an appeal is attempted in the following pages, with what success the reader must judge.

If the appeal is successful, two ends will be accomplished. First, the absolute authority of the Scriptures will be brought to bear against Slavery, in the minds of all those who regard them in the light of a Revelation of the will of God. Secondly, the Scriptures will be vindicated against the charge of sanctioning the terrible system of American Slavery. It is a fact well understood that many are fast loosing their confidence in the Scriptures, upon the assumption that they justify Slavery. To vindicate the Bible from such a charge, and to stop the tide of infidelity arising from this source, is an object worthier of higher gifts than those displayed in the following pages, yet the Author hopes his little volume may be found among the influences which shall hasten the overthrow of human bondage. With these views and his earnest prayers for the triumph of truth, he submits his work to the judgment of the candid reader.

THE AUTHOR

TABLE OF CONTENTS.

SECTION I.

SECTION II.

SECTION III.

SLAVERY EXAMINED

SECTION I.

SIN INHERENT IN SLAVERY.

It is important to define the question to be discussed before opening the argument. It does not follow that slavery is right because one man may rightfully be another man's servant.

Limited servitude or such as pertains to children in their minority, and persons under various limited contracts and obligations, is not meant in the following Treatise. It is admitted that one person may rightfully owe service to another person under various circumstances.

By slavery is meant, the system which reduces man to a chattel, and buys and sells him, and subjects him to the liabilities of other property, claiming the same right of property in the offspring by virtue of the right previously asserted to the parent. This is the system of American slavery, and against it and all other slavery involving the same principles, the following arguments are directed.

Slavery consisting in the right of property in man, with the usual incidents of that right must be morally wrong and sin in itself, for the following reasons.

ARGUMENT FIRST.

It is inconsistent with man's relation to God, and the obligations growing out of that relation.

Dr. Payne, in his " Elements of Moral Science," says :—

" Virtue as it regards man, is the conformity or harmony of his affections and actions with the various relations in which he has been placed—of which conformity the perfect intellect of God, guided in its exercise by his infinitely holy nature, is the only infallible judge."

If this be a correct definition of virtue, and we believe it is ; it follows, that man cannot rightfully sustain two relations at the same time, with both of which his affections and actions cannot harmonize ; which is the case with the relation that all men sustain to God, and the relation to *property*, to man with its usual incidents. The relations we sustain to God are various. He is our Creator, our Preserver, our Benefactor—He is the framer of our bodies and the Father of our spirits, and he is our Governor.

The quotation from Dr. Payne asserts that God is the judge of the conformity of man's affections and actions to his relations, and this judgment God has expressed in the first

great commandment, which reads as follows :—

"Thou shalt love the Lord thy God with
all thy heart, and with all thy soul, and with
all thy mind, and with all thy strength."
This commandment clearly lays such a claim
to the affections of the heart, and demands
such an entire devotion of the soul (*Psukee
Life*) as gives tone to, and controls the actions ; it therefore contains the foundation
of absolute obedience to God. This is seen
in the expression, "with all thy strength."
This requires a consecration of the physical
powers in obedience to God, under the control of the affections of the heart.

There is but one question more to settle,
which is, can these affections and *actions* exist in the same heart and life, at the same
time with those affections and *actions* which
are consonant with the relation of a piece of
property to its owner, a personal chattel to
a chattel holder ? Slavery may say what it
pleases ; common sense says no.

To be under obligation to obey God, there
must exist the right and power of devoting
our lives to God, for there can be no obligation where there is not both *right* and *power*
to respond to that obligation. But the slave,
who is the property of man, has not and
cannot have the power of devoting his life to
God, because his life is not at his own dis-
posal, according to the dictates of his own
understanding of right ; he cannot do what
God requires, but must do what *men require*,
and wicked men too, who fear not God and
regard not his law. Should it be said that

slave owners do not interfere with the slave's right to obey God, and liberty of conscience, every one must know that such an assumption would be false, for the extension of the right to slaves, to obey God, as free men professing the religion of the Bible deem it their duty to obey God, would overthrow the system of slavery.

Further, if it were admitted that slave owners grant their slaves the privilege of obeying God, it would not relieve the difficulty, for it would still follow that the system of property in man, takes away from the human chattel the *right* to obey God, and puts it into the hand of the owner, who has the power to close up before the chattelized traveller to eternity, the path of obedience and with authority direct his footsteps in the way of sin and death. Man cannot sustain the relation of property to man, without an infraction of the relation that he sustains to God, and of the rights and powers essential to the conformity of his affections and *actions* to this relation, hence, the *right* of property in man cannot exist.

The assumption of the relation of a chattel holder to a subject of God's moral government, is to step in between such subject and God, and disannul man's relation to his Maker, and absolve him from his allegiance to Jehovah's throne. Can this be right? Does the Bible sanction such a principle, beaming as it does with the mind of Him who declares himself to be a jealous God ; flashing with the lightnings of his displeasure, and speaking in the thunder tones of his wrath against all who turn away from the claims of his law to acknowledge any other authority, to serve any other God or bow down to the likeness of any thing in heaven, earth or hell? It cannot be.

ARGUMENT SECOND:

SLAVERY CONFLICTS WITH VARIOUS SPECIFIC DUTIES WHICH THE BIBLE REQUIRES OF ALL MEN.

Dr. Paley, in his moral philosophy, lays down the following rule :

"A state of happiness is not to be expected by those who reserve to themselves the habitual practice of any one sin, or the neglect of any one known duty."

If then it can be shown that a state of slavery does interfere with a single duty to God, or involves its subjects in the necessity of violating one single precept of the gospel it will follow that it is and must remain wrong under all circumstances and forever.

It is the duty of all intelligent beings to use all the means within their reach to acquire a knowledge of God and his will. To remain ignorant of God and of his will concerning us through neglect of the means within our reach, is of itself a sin of the darkest shade. But from what source is the knowledge of God to be derived? The answer is plain,

the *Scriptures.* "To the law and the testimony ; if they speak not according to this
word it is because there is no light in them."

It is clear that if the Scriptures are an expression of the mind of God, and have been
inspired by his spirit, all must possess a common right of direct access to this fountain of
moral light.   This none will deny but the
Pope and his menials.   With this accords
the practice of all Protestants ; whenever
they establish missions in any part of the
world among the heathen, they put the Bible
into their hands so soon as they can speak
its language, or so soon as it can be translated into their own language.   The only exception is found in the act of withholding
the scriptures from the slaves of our own
country, who might be taught to read them
with far greater facility.

But God has made it our duty to know
him, and to know him through this medium.

Luke xvi. 29.   "They have Moses and
the prophets ; let them hear them."

John v. 39.   "Search the scriptures, for
in them ye think he have eternal life."

Acts xvii. 11.   " These were more no-
ble than those in Thessalonica, in that they
received the word with all readiness of mind,
and searched the scriptures daily, whether
these things were so."

W. M. Discipline—" It is expected of all
who desire to continue in these societies,
that they should continue to evidence their
desire of salvation BY SEARCHING THE SCRIP-
TURES.   All this we know his spirit writes

on truly awakened hearts. All which we are taught of God to observe."

The same principle is contained in the creed, written or unwritten, of every Protestant religious sect on earth ; and every Protestant sect condemn the Romanists for withholding the scriptures from the people ; and if it be wrong to withhold the scriptures. slavery cannot be right.

The right and duty of all men to possess themselves of the scriptures and to read and study the same being established, it only remains to show that slavery is of necessity and forever inimical to this right and duty ; taking away the one, and nullifying the other. The right of property in man cannot exist co-ordinate with the right and obligation to ' search the scriptures.'

1. The right and obligation to search the scriptures necessarily includes the right of acquiring property, first in money or money's value with which to procure the scriptures to be read : and secondly, in the scriptures themselves. But property cannot acquire property ; the very idea of the right of property in any thing, supposes an equal right of properity in all productions and increase or income of such property; so that property cannot acquire property in its own right and for itself. If property increases or gathers other property around it, such increase does not belong to the property that produces or acquires it, but to the owner of the property. If this be denied, it will follow that the productions of the slaves do not belong to the slave owner but the slave him-

self, which will overthrow the whole system
of slavery. This view shows that the slave,
as property, cannot possess, in his own right,
a Bible or the value of a Bible in any form,
and therefore, the command of God to 'search
the scriptures,' and the assumed right of property in man, are totally and irreconcilably
opposed to each other, so that while God requires all men to search the scriptures, no
man can rightfully be reduced to a chattel.
With this agrees the law of slavery which
says that a slave " can do nothing, possess
nothing, nor acquire anything but what must
belong to their master." If a Bible should
be given to a slave, so as to alienate the right
of the giver in favor of the slave, the right
to the Bible would not lodge with the slave,
but pass over him and vest itself with the
master, and this is not only by law but in
the very philosophy of the right of property.

2. The right and obligation to search the
scriptures includes the right to devote sufficient time to the pursuit of religious knowledge. But the right of property in a man
includes the right to monopolize and dispose
of his whole time, so that he cannot possess
the right of devoting his time or any part of
it to the study of the scriptures, from which
it follows again that the right of slavery is
at war with the duties which God has commanded. If the advocate of slavery will attempt to evade the force of this, by denying
that the right of property in man includes
the right to control the time of such property, he will ruin his own cause; for if the

slaveholder has not a right to say how the slave shall improve his time, his right of property in him will not be worth contending about. If the right of property in man includes the right of controling his time, it conflicts with duties which God requires and must be wrong ; and if it does not give the master the right to control the time of the slave, the whole practical system of slavery is a violation of right.

In showing that slavery conflicts with certain specified duties, it is proper to notice the duty of publicly worshipping God. On this point we will quote but one text.

Heb. x. 25. "Not forsaking the assembling of yourselves together, as the manner of some is." This text clearly teaches the duty of meeting together in Christian assemblies for religious purposes, while slavery declares that the right of slaves so to assemble cannot be admitted with safety to the system.

To conclude this argument, we say that to grant the slaves the simple *right of obeying the Gospel*, by attending to all its devotional and social *duties as they are commanded and understood by Christians generally*, would *overthrow the entire system*. To give them the Scriptures to be read according to the dictates of their own consciences, and to allow them the privilege of *selecting their own ministers* from whose lips they choose to hear the words of life, which is the inalienable right of all Christians, would come so near to the abolition of slavery as to leave but little to be done to complete it. The *right of proper-*

ty in man cannot exist without taking away the *right of doing the duties and enjoying the privileges of the Gospel,* and therefore the right of property in man cannot exist *as a right,* but must be *wrong,* whenever assumed.

ARGUMENT THIRD:

SLAVERY CONFLICTS WITH THOSE SOCIAL RE-
LATIONS AND DUTIES WHICH NOT ONLY SPRING FROM
OUR SOCIAL NATURE, BUT WHICH GOD HAS ALSO EN-
JOINED BY POSITIVE ENACTMENT.

Man is a social being, and has received a social nature from the hand which formed him; which seeks intercourse, sympathy, and reciprocal enjoyments from kindred spirits. The various relations into which we are thrown by the current of our social nature, have been provided for by God in his word, where he has prescribed the circumstances, conditions and obligations of our social and domestic relations, and has thrown around them the protection of his law.

We will commence with the institution of marriage. This of course was provided for by the hand of God when he originally created man, and is the first institution in the chain of social relations ; first in the order of nature, and first in the order of the positive institutions of the divine law. **Matt. xix. 4--6.**

"Have ye not read that he which made them at the beginning, made them male and female, and said, For this cause shall a man leave father and mother, and shall cleave to his wife, and they twain shall be one flesh? Wherefore they are no more twain but one flesh? what therefore God hath joined together let no man put asunder."

Heb. xiii. "Marriage is honorable in all, and the bed undefiled ; but whoremongers and adulterers God will judge."

On these texts it may be remarked, that God obviously designed marriage for all nations, races and classes of men. To say that God does not require marriage on the part of the African race, would be to say that he designs the extinction of the race, for all such perpetuation of the race out of wedlock is condemned and denounced by God himself. We are now prepared to show wherein slavery conflicts with the institution, and rights and obligations of marriage.

1. The right of property in man is inconsistent with the rights of the parties who lawfully enter into the marriage relation.

The husband has a monopoly of right in his wife. A wife belongs to her husband, in a sense which renders it impossible that she should be the property of another at the same time ; if she is the wife of one, she cannot be the property of another ; if she is the property of one she cannot be the wife of another. It is impossible from the nature of the two things that a woman should hold out the attributes of a wife to one man, and the attributes of property to another, at the

same time. The husband has an exclusive
right in his wife, and the owner has an exclusive right in his property ; hence, a woman cannot sustain the relation of a wife to
one man, and the relation of property to another. The husband has not only an exclusive claim to the affections of her heart, but
also to her time and attention ; what power
she possesses to promote the happiness of another belongs to him, and she has, as a wife,
no right to seek the happiness of others beyond what is consistent with his happiness ;
her happiness should be his and 'his should be
hers ; they are partners in both joy and sorrow ; " they are no more twain but one flesh."
The right of property includes the right of
controlling, using, and disposing of such
property for the promotion of the happiness
of the owner ; hence, two persons cannot
possess,. the one the rights of a husband and
the other the rights of property in the same
woman at the same time. In the same manner the rights of the wife forever forbid the
right of property in the husband. The man
is not alone in securing rights to himself
when he enters into the marriage relation ;
corresponding to his rights are the rights of
the wife ; if they are not in every respect
the same, they are nevertheless equal in number and importance. The husband is bound
no less to devote himself for the promotion
of the happiness of the wife than she is to
promote his happiness. This right of the
wife to the love, the protection, the support,
and entire devotedness of the husband to
promote her happiness must forever preclude

the right of property to such husband vest-
ing itself in the hands of another.

2. The right of property in man is inconsistent with the obligations resting upon the
parties to the marriage relations.   Rights
and obligations are always reciprocal; hence,
in treating of the rights of the parties, the
corresponding obligations have been implied,
but we wish to bring them out a little more
distinctly.   The right of the husband to the
due regard and proper submission of the
wife, involves an obligation on her part to
render these things; the right of the wife to
the love and protection of the husband, involves an obligation on his part to love and
protect her.   We will now present a few
plain declarations of scripture on this subject, and see how effectually they overthrow
the assumed right of property in man.

1 Cor. vii. 2.   " Nevertheless, *to avoid* for
nication, let every man have his own wife,
and let every woman have her own husband."

The system of property in man, making
them personal chattels, to be bought and
sold in the market, cannot be reconciled
with the above text.   To let every man have
his own wife, and every woman her own husband, in the apostle's sense, would overthrow
the whole system of slavery.

Eph. v. 21.   " Wives submit yourselves
unto your own husbands, as unto the Lord.

23. For the husband is the head of the
wife, even as Christ is the head of the church:
and he is the Saviour of the body."

Can wives, who are the personal chattels

of men not their husbands, comply with the
above text ?   When the husband is sent to
one market and the wife to another, can the
wife obey the scriptures ?   Can the wife who
is in the power, the absolute power of a man
who is not her husband, and who can enforce
his will in all things without let or hindrance
by flattery, bribes, strength, prisons, whips
and tortures ; can such a wife submit herself
to her husband as unto the Lord ? and can a
husband, who is under the same absolute control of another, be the head of such a wife,
as Christ is the head of the church ?   Answer, common sense !

1 Cor. vii. 10.   " And unto the married
I command, *yet* not I, but the Lord, Let not
the wife depart from her husband ?"

Is it consistent with this text for one man
to sell another man's wife, or to buy another
man's wife, and drive her off in chains, to
see her husband no more ?   It cannot be. If
the wife has not a right to depart, then no
other person can have a right to force her to
depart.   No person can have a right to compel another to do what such person has not
a right to do without being compelled.   A
wife has no power to depart from her husband, and therefore no person can have a
right to sell her, to buy and drive her away
from her husband ; and hence the right of
property in husbands and wives cannot exist.

Eph. v. 28.   " So ought men to love their
wives as their own bodies.   He that loveth
his wife loveth himself.

29. For no man ever yet hated his own

flesh ; but nourisheth and cherisheth it, even
as the Lord the church ?"

1 Peter iii. 7. "Likewise, ye husbands,
dwell with *them* according to knowledge,
giving honor unto the wife, as unto the weak-
er vessel, and as being heirs together of the
grace of life ; that your prayers be not hin-
dered."

How can a man, who may be sold and driv-
en away at any moment, be under obligation
to dwell with his wife?   We will not multiply quotations or remarks ; enough has been
said to show that slavery and the marriage
institution cannot exist together.   Slavery
takes away the power of the wife to preserve
her own purity, and this is true of married
and unmarried females.   The female that is
made an article of property, cannot call her
purity her own ; it may be taken from her at
the pleasure of her owner.   He may violate
her at pleasure, and she has neither the right
or the power to resist.   He may tie her up
with cords ; he may confine her in any way
he pleases ; he may apply the lash to her
cringing back to any extent he pleases ; and
all this he may do before the face of the man
she may call her husband, and no one, bond
or free, has any right to interfere ; and in so
doing he violates no law but the law of God,
with which slavery has nothing to do more
than to set it at nought.

All this follows of necessity, from the ad-
mission of the right of property in human
beings. Note, the argument is not that all
slaveholders actually commit these wrongs
on the marriage institution and on female

purity, but the argument is that the system of slavery gives every slaveholder the power to do it at pleasure, and with perfect impunity ; and that this is inseparable from the system itself ; and that the system which lays the heaven ordained institution of marriage, and heaven-protected female virtue in the dust, helpless at the feet of the spoiler, for the riot and triumph of the baser passions of human nature, cannot be right, but must be wrong now and forever.

To settle the question, we say that matrimony exists among slaves or it does not.— The one or the other of these positions must be true.   Which is true, we care not, so far as this argument is concerned.   1. If matrimony does exist in moral right among slaves, the parties are joined together by God, and Christ says, " what God hath joined together, let not man put asunder."   But slavery does sunder them, and the right of property includes the right of sundering them.   If therefore slaves are married in moral right, slavery is guilty of parting those whom God had joined together, and drags after it the crime of adultery.   The slave system separates the parties and joins them in other connections, so that within a few years the same man may have several wives, and the same woman several husbands, and all living at the same time.

2. If slaves are not married in moral right, as they are not and cannot be in the eyes of the civil law, slavery stands charged with breaking up this heaven appointed institution, and of involving the slave population

in the crime of general whoredom. There
is so far as we can see, no way to escape
these conclusions ; if the advocate of slavery
allows that slaves are brought within the
marriage institution, he assumes that the
power to separate those whom God hath
joined together can rightfully exist ; a thing,
in our view, impossible. If he admits that
slaves are not brought within the marriage
institution, he assumes the rightfulness of
general sexual intercourse without the bans
of matrimony. Such is slavery, consisting
in the assumed right of property in human
beings, wherever it is found, in the church
or out of the church. We speak as to wise
men ; judge of what we say.

ARGUMENT FOURTH:

SLAVERY FURTHER CONFLICTS WITH THOSE SOCIAL RELATIONS AND DUTIES WHICH NOT ONLY SPRING FROM OUR SOCIAL NATURE, BUT WHICH GOD HAS ALSO EN-JOINED BY POSITIVE ENACTMENT BY SUBVERTING THE RIGHTS AND OBLIGATIONS WHICH GROW OUT OF RELATIONS SUBSISTING BETWEEN PARENTS AND CHILD-REN.

That there are rights and obligations con-nected with this relation, around which God has thrown the protection of his law, armed with the arrows of his lightnings, and the voice of his thunders, cannot be denied ; and that slavery disregards them and tramples them under foot, if not admitted shall be proved.

When God descended upon Mount Sinai and gave his law amid the dreadful light-nings that blazed and glared, and shot their fiery arrows athwart the smoke and gloom that mantled the Eternal upon the mount, and amid the thunders that bellowed terrors and poured the voice of condemnation in the ear of sin ; He then wrote with his own finger upon a table of stone, as the fifth of the ten commandments, the following words : " Honor thy father and mother, that thy days may be-long upon the land which the Lord thy God giveth thee."

The duty of the child to honor his father and mother, clearly implies the obligation of the parents so to teach and so to behave towards the child, as is calculated to inspire the feelings and write upon the heart of the child what God wrote in the book of his law. This sentiment is clearly brought out in the comment of St. Paul.

" Ephe. vi. 1--4. " Children obey your parents in the Lord for this is right. Honor thy father and mother which is the first commandment with promise, that it may be well with thee, and thou mayest live long on the earth. And ye, fathers, provoke not your children to wrath ; but bring them up in the nurture and admonition of the Lord.

Here we have the obligation growing out of the relation that subsists between parents and children, as defined by the spirit of inspiration ; and that slavery necessarily wars upon, and entirely subverts these obligations, is all that remains to be proved, and this is so plain and obvious that it is like proving what is self evident.

1. Can parents, who are subject to all the liabilities of property, and whose children are also property in the same full sense, bring up their children in the nurture and admonition of the Lord ? This cannot be pretended. Sons are torn away from the embrace of their father, and removed forever beyond the sight of his eye ; daughters are borne in chains from the throbbing, heaving bosom and bleeding hearts of their mothers.

" Where no mother's ear can hear them,
Where no mother's eye can see them."

Slavery which assumes the right of property in man, in fathers and mothers, and mothers and children, takes from the parents all right of control over their children, and

hence, it violates the divine law, for that
commands them to control them for good.
God says to parents, " bring up your children
in the nurture and admonition of the Lord ;"
but slavery says, no, you cannot have the
right of bringing them up, or if you do, you
must bring them up for the market, bring
them up for me, that I may sacrifice your
sons upon the altar of my avarice, and your
daughters upon the altar of my lust.

2. Can children who are " personal chattels
to all intents and purposes and constructions
whatsoever," honor their fathers and mothers ?   Can they " obey their parents in the
Lord ?"   Most certainly not.   The son looks
not, cannot look to his father, if father he
knows, for authority and direction during
the years of his minority ; nor can he honor,
comfort, and support that father in his declin-
ing years, after the son has come to the riper
years of manhood.   The daughter cannot
obey her own mother in childhood and youth,
much less can she honor and cherish her in
riper years ; she must see her mother, if she
be allowed to see her at all, languish, faint
and die under the effects of toil, hunger and
the lash, without dropping a word of conso-
lation in her ear, or extending a daughter's
hand to her relief—all this is true of the
daughter, concerning her who in anguish gave
her being, and sheltered her in her bosom
during the cloudy morning of her existence,
and nourished her upon the milk of toil and
weariness until she was strong enough to endure life's heavier storms.

That all this is wicked, it would be an in-

sult to common sense to attempt to prove.
It directly violates and sets aside as plain a
command as there is in the book of God, and
if this is not sin, the ten commandments may
all be violated without sin.

Should it be said in reply to this, that under the circumstances, the parents are released from the obligation to bring up their
children in the nurture and admonition of the
Lord, and children are released from the obligation to obey their parents in the Lord,
as God's law does not require impossibilities ;
we respond, that God's law can never be
annihilated or nullified in its claims.   It is and
must forever be, binding in some form ; and
if the above circumstances exempt parents and
children from the obligation to obey God's
law, or rather from the penalty of the law,
for it is not obeyed, the guilt rests upon
those who are the authors of such circumstances.   If a man who is stronger than we
put fetters upon us so that we cannot do
what God has commanded us to do, God will
not, it is true, hold us responsible ; but he
will hold that man responsible who puts the
fetters upon us for the non performance of
all that duty, of which he has been the cause.
When the slaveholder steps in between God
and the slave, and between parents and children, to prevent the discharge of the duties
which God commands them as parents and
children to discharge towards each other, he
takes the place of both parent and child, and
assumes before God the responsibility of the
non-performance of the duty of both, for
which God will hold him responsible.   This

argument might be greatly extended, and the
terrible consequences to society, resulting
from a dissolution of all social relations and
ties, might be dwelt upon, but it is not necessary. The simple fact that it conflicts with
the specific commands of God secures all that
is to be gained by the argument.

ARGUMENT FIFTH.

THE BIBLE CONDEMNS SLAVERY UNDER THE NAME OF MAN-STEALING.

It would be a waste of time to attempt to prove that man-stealing is a crime. It is universally admitted that all stealing is wrong, and it follows that man-stealing is the most sinful of all theft. It cannot be maintained that to steal the horse under the rider would be a sin, while to steal the rider off the horse would be a justifiable act.

That man-stealing is condemned in the Bible will not be denied. Ex. xxi. 16. " He that stealeth a man and selleth him, or if he be found in his hand, shall surely be put to death." St. Paul tells us, 2 Tim. i. 10, that the law of God " is made for men stealers." The only question about which there can be any dispute is this ; is American slavery, as it now exists, man-stealing ?

I. American slavery had its origin in man-stealing.

1. The facts, as generally understood, are such as to stamp the whole business of the foreign slave trade with the odious name of man-stealing. No matter who was engaged in it, saint or devil, it was nevertheless man-stealing. The business commenced by stealing such persons as they could catch along the coast, and force away from country,

home and friends, to live, suffer and die in
bondage among strangers. When the increasing market could not be supplied in this
way, other means were resorted to. The
kidnappers would land for purposes of trade,
and while trading, would pour out to their
unsuspecting customers the intoxicating drink,
who, not being acquainted with the power of
ardent spirit, would soon become helpless,
and then while drunk the pale-faced demons
would secure them. When they awoke from
their drunkenness, they found themselves, not
like Noah under the protection of affection-
ate sons, but in chains and in the hell of the
slave ship. But at last, to supply the increasing demand, war was resorted to, which
was no less man-stealing. The wars, it
should be understood, were commenced for the
express purpose of obtaining slaves, hence, it
was stealing on a larger scale. If two men
go and take one, it is stealing ; if ten go and
take five, it is stealing ; if one hundred go
and take fifty, it is stealing ; and if one thousand go and take five hundred, it is no less
man-stealing.

2. The law of our country deems it man-
stealing. It is pronounced piracy, and punished by death by the laws of the United
States. It is no more morally wrong now,
than when it was tolerated : hence, it was
always wrong.

II. The present race or generation of
slaves can be held by no better title or authority than that by which their stolen fathers and mothers were held. They were
originally stolen, and, of course, there was

no valid title to them ; if, therefore, there is now a title to those bondmen and bond-women, it has been obtained or originated since their fathers and mothers were stolen. We demand at what period in the dark history of slavery, this supposed title to these human beings began to exist. As there was no title at first, they being stolen, it follows that there can be no title now, that they are stolen persons still, unless it can be shown when, under what circumstances, and upon what principles the title originated, and began to exist.

By the law of slavery, the condition of the offspring follows the condition of the mother. Let us then suppose what is the fact in the case,—some men-stealers, for whom the law of God was made, went to Africa, and stole a helpless female. Had he any right or title to her? Certainly not. The next step in this infamous business was, the man-thief sold this stolen female to a Southern planter. Had the planter any title to her? Certainly not ; for he could have none only what he bought; and he could buy none only what the thief had to sell ; and he had no title to sell, and therefore he could sell none ; and therefore the planter could buy none of him ; and therefore the planter could have no title. This is all just as certain as it is that one man cannot communicate to another what he has not got. As the thief had no title to his stolen victim, he could communicate no title to the man to whom he sold.

The third step in the progress of slavery

is, this enslaved female had offspring in her
bonds. Had the planter, who held her without title, a title to her child as his property ?
Slavery itself does not pretend to any title
to the children which is not founded upon a
supposed title to the mother ; hence, as
there was no title to the mother, there can
be none to the child. As the mother was a
stolen person in his hands, so is the child a
stolen person in his hands if he restrains it
as his property. Slavery, therefore, is man-
stealing, and must remain man-stealing so
long as it shall be continued.

It can make no difference in moral principle, from what particular place we steal a
human being, whether from Africa or in
America. Now, it appears, from the boast-
ed chart of the nation's rights, that every
child, born in this land, has an inalienable
right to liberty, as much so as children now
born in Africa or in any other country.
Where, then, is the difference in moral principle, whether we go to Africa and take a
child, and bring it here for a slave, or take
one born here ? The child, born of the enslaved mother in South Carolina, has the
same inalienable right to liberty, the gift of
God, as the child born in Africa. Where is
the justice ? Where is the consistency ? If
the law of the nation, which declares that
he who brings children from Africa to make
slaves of them, shall be hanged as a pirate
upon the high seas, be right, then he who
takes children born in this land, and holds
them as property and as slaves, ought to be
hanged as a land pirate ; for the one has the

same inalienable right to liberty as the other.

To invalidate these arguments, we must deny the truth of the Declaration of American Independence, we must disprove the unity of human nature, that " God has made of one blood all nations of men," equal in natural rights ; and we must falsify the universal conviction of mankind, which each feels, that he was born free, and has a right to himself.

We will close this argument by saying that American slavery is essentially man-stealing ; that the Bible condemns man-stealing, and therefore theBible condemns slavery.

ARGUMENT SIXTH:

THE BIBLE FURTHER CONDEMNS SLAVERY SPECIFICALLY BY CONDEMNING THE TRAFFIC IN HUMAN BEINGS.

Deut. xxiv. 7. "If a man be found stealing any of his brethren of the children of Israel, and maketh merchandise of him, or selleth him ; then that thief shall die ; and thou shalt put evil away from among you."

This text most clearly condemns, not only the act of stealing men, but the act of making merchandize of men. The principle of traffic in human beings is condemned. There is only one point on which the advocate of slavery can hang an objection and that is the

fact that it simply condemns making merchandise of the children of Israel. This is
fully answered by the remark that Israel
after the flesh, cannot be more sacred in the
eye of God, than Israel after the Spirit. If
it was wrong to make merchandise of a Jew,
because he was a Jew, it must be wrong to
make merchandise of a Christian, because
he is a Christian.

Chap xxi. 14. "And it shall be, if thou
have no delight in her, then thou shalt let
her go whither she will ; but thou shalt not
sell her for money, thou shalt not make merchandise of her."

This is spoken of a female captive taken
in war, it fully condemns the idea of selling
human beings.

Amos ii. 6. "Thus saith the Lord ; For
three transgressions of Israel, and for four,
I will not turn away *the punishment* thereof ;
because they sold the righteous for silver,
and the poor for a pair of shoes."

On this text it may be remarked.

1. The slaves are often *righteous*, so that it
is true to the very letter, that the righteous
are sold for silver.

2. The slaves are all *poor* and are often
bartered and gambled away for a consideration as small as a pair of shoes.

Zech. xi. 4, 5. "Thus saith the Lord my
God ; Feed the flock of the slaughter, whose
possessors slay them, and hold themselves
not guilty : and they that sell them say,
Blessed *be* the Lord ; for I am rich : and
their own shepherds pity them not."

If there was ever a true picture, this is a

true picture of slavery : The members of the flock of Jesus Christ are sold, " and they that sell them say blessed be the Lord, for I am rich ; and their own shepherds pity them not."

Joel iii. 3. " And they have cast lots for my people ; and have given a boy for a harlot, and sold a girl for wine, that they might drink."

That every crime here condemned is part and parcel of American slavery, cannot be denied. The right of property in man is the foundation of these crimes. How often are slaves exchanged one for another, so that it is literally true that a boy is given for a harlot. Again, how often is it the case in their gambling and drinking revels that slaveholders pawn their servants for their bills, or gamble them away, so that it is literally true that a girl is sold for wine that they may drink.

In concluding this argument, two things are to be noticed.

1. The Bible, as has been shown, clearly condemns the traffic in human beings.

2. American slavery assumes the right of buying and selling human beings as personal chattles.

From the above propositions it follows that the Bible condemns slavery.

ARGUMENT SEVENTH:

THE BIBLE FURTHER CONDEMNS SLAVERY SPECIFI-
CALLY BY CONDEMNING INVOLUNTARY SERVITUDE.

That slavery is involuntary servitude will
not be denied : Indeed it is only involuntary slavery that we labor to condemn in
these numbers.   The only question that needs
to be settled in this argument, is the wrong
of forcing one man to serve another against
his will.   We know of no scriptures, which,
by any fair construction, can be made to justify compulsory service.   But we will quote
a few texts which, in our own mind, condemn
it.

Deut. xxiii. 15, 16.—" Thou shalt not deliver unto his master the servant which is
escaped from his master unto thee ; He shall
dwell with thee, even among you, in that
place which he shall choose in one of thy
gates, where it liketh him best ; thou shalt
not oppress him."

This text most clearly condemns involuntary service, for it most clearly justifies the
servant in leaving his master and protects
him in it against the pursuits of his master,
and even forbids the people among whom he
may go to deliver him up.   It appears from
this text that there was such a thing as involuntary servitude, and in this text it is effectually condemned.   It is clear that the
Jews were forbidden to compel service
against the will of the servant.   This will
appear still more plain from another text.
This subject is treated at large by the pro-

phet, and to save the reader the trouble of turning to his Bible, while reading this argument, we quote the prophet at length.

Jer. xxxiv. 6. " Then Jeremiah the prophet spake all these words unto Zedekiah king of Judah in Jerusalem :

7. When the king of Babylon's army fought against Jerusalem, and against all the cities of Judah that were left, against Lachish, and against Azekah ; for these defenced cities remained of the cities of Judah.

8. This is the word that came unto Jeremiah from the Lord, after that the king Zedekiah had made a covenant with all the people which were at Jerusalem, to proclaim liberty unto them ;

9. That every man should let his man servant, and every man his maid servant, being a Hebrew or a Hebrewess, go free ; that none should serve himself of them ; and to wit, of a Jew his brother.

10. Now when all the princes and all the people, which had entered into the covenant, heard that every one should let his man servant, and every one his maid servant, go free that none should serve themselves of them any more, then they obeyed, and let them go.

11. But afterwards they turned and caused the servants and the hand maids, whom they had let go free, to return, and brought them into subjection for servants and for hand maids.

12. Therefore the word of the Lord came to Jeremiah from the Lord, saying,

13. Thus saith the Lord, the God of Is-

rael ; I made a covenant with your fathers
in the day that I brought them forth out of
the house of bondmen, saying,

14. At the end of seven years let ye go
every man his brother a Hebrew, which hath
been sold unto thee ; and when he hath served thee six years, thou shalt let him go free
from thee : but your fathers hearkened not
unto me, neither inclined their ear.

15. And ye were now turned, and had
done right in my sight, in proclaiming liberty to every man to his neighbor ; and ye
had made a covenant before me in the house
which is called by my name :

16. But ye turned and polluted my name,
and caused every man his servant, and every
man his hand maid, whom he had set at liberty at their pleasure, to return, and brought
them into subjection, to be unto you for servants and for hand maids.

16. Therefore thus saith the Lord ; ye
have not hearkened unto me, in proclaiming
liberty every one to his brother, and every
man to his neighbor : behold, I proclaim a
liberty for you, saith the Lord, to the sword,
to the pestilence, and to the famine ; and I
will make you to be removed into all the
kingdoms of the earth."

The fourteenth verse speaks of being sold
for seven years, but it is obvious the price
for which a man was sold was his own, and
went into his own pocket, for the benefit of
his family, or at most to pay his debts, the
amount of which he-had previously enjoyed
and consumed. What is here called selling
was obviously nothing more than a contract

for service with pay in advance ; and hence the law was like our statute of limitation. It forbade men to make a contract for service for more than seven years. The seven years' service was voluntary, because agreed upon by the parties, and paid for in advance ; but when they kept the servant beyond that time, it became involuntary, and God condemned it, and punished them for it.

Isa. lviii. 6. " *Is* not this the fast that I have chosen ? to loose the bands of wickedness, to undo the heavy burdens, and to let the oppressed go free ?"

The expression, " let the oppressed *go free,*" is a full condemnation of involuntary servitude. To compel any man to serve another against his will, who is out of his minority and uncondemned for crime, is to oppress him ; and the command to let the oppressed go *free*, condemns such forced service.

American slavery is a system of force and violence, and cannot be maintained for a day, only by a constant war upon the very life of the slaves. For all this there is no warrant in the Bible, but much against it. Involuntary service must be wrong, from the fact that the violence necessary to maintain it is wrong. Whips for the naked back, thumb screws, chains, prisons, and other modes of torture, to subdue persons unconvicted of crime, have no warrant in the Gospel, and cannot be justified, only upon a principle which will justify every species of violence men may choose to practice one upon another.

ARGUMENT EIGHTH.

SLAVERY IS A WORK WITHOUT WAGES, WHICH IS CON-
DEMNED IN THE BIBLE.

Deut. xxiv. 14, 15. "Thou shalt not oppress a hired servant that is poor and needy,
whether he be of thy brethren, or of thy
strangers that be in thy land within thy
gates. At his day thou shalt give him his
hire, neither shall the sun go down upon it ;
for he is poor, and setteth his heart upon it ;
lest he cry against thee unto the Lord, and
it be sin unto the."

It may be said that this text does not meet
the case, because it speaks of hired servant,
but this cannot alter the principle involved.
The text condemns the act of withholding
what is a man's due for his labor, and this
every slaveholder does. One man voluntarily goes to work with the expectation of
wages, while the employer seizes upon another and compels him to work, *nolens volens*.
We ask is not the man who is compelled to
work as much entitled to pay as he who
works voluntarily ? Certainly he is. This
is kept back, and in this the slave is oppressed.

Jer. xxii. 13, 14. " Wo unto him that build-
eth his house by unrighteousness, and his
chambers by wrong ; that useth his neigh-

bor's service without wages, and giveth him
not for his work ; that saith, I will build me
a wide house and a large chambers, and cut-
teth him out windows ; and it is ceiled with
cedar, and painted with vermilion."

This most certainly meets the case exactly ;
nothing is said about hiring men, but simply
using their service without wages, which
every slaveholder does.   Men are here absolutely forbidden to use their neighbor's service without wages, and as slavery is a system of work without wages, it is here forbidden.

Hab. ii. 9, 10, 11, 12. "Wo to him that
coveteth an evil covetousness to his house,
that he may set his nest on high, that he
may be delivered from the power of evil !
Thou hast consulted shame to thy house by
cutting off many people, and hast sinned
against thy soul.   For the stone shall cry
out of the wall, and the beam out of the tim-
ber shall answer it.   Wo to him that build-
eth a town with blood, and establisheth a
city by iniquity.

To establish a city by iniquity is to build
up a city with the fruit of the unpaid toil of
slaves, and every city in the south is built
in this way.

Mal. iii. 5. "And I will come near to you
to judgment : and I will be a swift witness
against the sorcerers, and against abulterers,
and against false swearers, and against those
who oppress the hireling in his wages, the
widow and the fatherless, and that turn aside
the stranger from his right, and fear not me
saith the Lord of hosts."

James v. 4. " Behold, the hire of the laborers which have reaped down your fields,
which is of you kept back by fraud, crieth ;
and the cries of them which have reaped are
entered into the ears of the Lord of Sabaoth."

The above texts are sufficient to prove that
the Bible forbids one class of men to use the
labor of another class, without paying them
for their work, and in forbidding this, it forbids slavery. Some may say that slaves are
paid in food and raiment. These are bestowed only so far as they promote the master's
interest, and they are not wages any more
than the oats a man feeds his horse, or the
grease he puts upon his carriage, or the ma-
nure with which he dresses his field, are
wages. Wages is the amount stipulated and
paid for service, but there is no stipulation
between the master and slave ; the slave has
no voice in determining the amount he receives ; this is unknown to him at the time
labor is demanded and rendered, and is determined by the arbitrary will of the master.
to constitute wages, the amount rendered for
service must be a matter of mutual agreement
between the parties. But as slavery is a system of absolute rule on the part of the master, and of coerced submission on the part of
the slave, without the consent of his will to
condition or stipulation, the very idea of
wages is excluded.

ARGUMENT NINTH.

THE BIBLE CONDEMNS SLAVERY UNDER THE NAME OF OPPRESSION.

Two points are to be settled, ʼviz., that slavery is identical with oppression, and how the Bible treats oppression.

What is oppresson ? According to Dr. Webster, oppression is "the imposition of unreasonable burdens, either in taxes or service." An oppressor, according to the same authority, is "one that imposes unjust burdens on others ; one that harasses others with unjust laws or unreasonable severity." This is a life like picture of slavery and slaveholders. It must be the extreme of oppression. For one man, because he has the power so to do, to compel his neighbor to work for him twenty-five days in a year, without his consent, would be oppression, and will it not be oppression to compel him to work the whole year ? If slavery be not oppression, than may an evil be changed to a virtue by increasing it in magnitude. To compel a man to work without wages every tenth year of his life, would be oppression by univeral consent, but to compel him to work life-long, commencing his toils at the misty dawn of existence, and closing them amid the gathering shadows of its dark going down, is no oppression ! According to this logic, to rob a man of a part of his la-

bor would be wrong, but to take the whole
would make it right!   To rob a man of a
part of his time, would be a crime, but to rob
him of all his time, of himself, his head and
heart, his body and limbs, his mind and will,
and all he can do, possess and acquire, renders it an act of righteousness!

But the Bible will settle the question of
oppression.

Ex. iii. 9. "Now therefore, behold, the cry
of the children of Israel is come unto me :
and I have also seen the oppression wherewith the Egyptians oppress them."

What then did the Egyptians do to the Israelites ?   They compelled them to work for
the government.

Here we have the history of the matter, as
follows :—Ex. i. 8–11. " Now there arose
up a new king over Egypt, which knew not
Joseph.   And he said unto his people, Behold, the people of the children of Israel *are*
more and mightier than we :   Come on, let
us deal wisely with them ; lest they multiply,
and it come to pass, that, when there falleth
out any war, they join also unto our enemies,
and fight against us, and so get them up out
of the land.   Therefore they did set over-
them task-masters, to afflict them with their
burdens.   And they built for Pharaoh trea-
sure-cities, Pithom and Raamses."

This was oppression which awakened the
sympathies of Jehovah, and brought out the
thickest and heaviest of his thunders.   Yet
he bore it longer than American slavery has
existed.   But what was there in that more
enormous than American slvery ?   Absolute-

ly nothing. They placed task-masters over them, and so do they place task masters over the slaves. And if, as a last resort, the Egyptians ordered the children of the Hebrews to be destroyed ; the slaveholders claim the children of the slaves as their property, and sell them in the market for gain, which is worse than to be strangled at birth. It is clear that slavery is oppression of the worst degree.

But how does God deal with oppression, and oppressors ? He condemns oppression and oppressors ; he commands his people to relieve the oppressed ; he threatens oppressors with terrible punishment, and has already expended more of his thunders, and more of the phials of his wrath on the heads of oppressors than on all other sinners.

Gen. xxv. 17. Ye shall not therefore oppress one another ; but thou shalt fear thy God : for I *am* the LORD thy God."

Here oppression is not only forbidden, but it is done in a manner which implies that it is inconsistent with the fear of God.

Deut. xxxiii. 15, 16. Thou shalt not deliver unto his master the servant which is escaped from his master unto thee : He shall dwell with thee, *even* among you, in that place which he shall choose in one of thy gates, where it liketh him best : thou shalt not oppress him." This clearly forbids the oppression of a self emancipated servant.

Deut. xxiv. 14. Thou shalt not oppress a hired servant that *is* poor and needy, *whether he be* of thy brethern, or of thy strangers that *are* in thy land within thy gates :"

This text specially forbids the oppression of a servant'that is a Jew or a Gentile.

Psal. x. 17, 18. "Lord, thou hast heard the desire of the humble, thou wilt prepare their heart, thou wilt cause thine ear to hear. To judge the fatherless and the oppressed, that the man of the earth may no more oppress." This appears to look forward to a day when oppression shall cease from the earth. Will there be any slavery there ?

Psa. lxxiii. 8, 9. " They are corrupt and speak wickedly *concerning* oppression : they speak loftily. They set their mouth against the heavens : and their tongue walketh through the earth. A clearer description could not well be given of modern slaveholders, and their abetters ; they speak wickedly concerning oppression. They invade the rights and government of God ; they set their mouth against the heavens.

Psa. xii. 5. "For the oppression of the poor, for the sighing of the needy, now will I arise saith the Lord ; I will set *him* in safety *from him that* puffeth at him."

Psa. lxxii. 4. "He shall judge the poor of the people, he shall save the children of the needy, and shall break in pieces the oppressor."

Isa. i. 17. Learn to do well : seek judgment, relieve the oppressed ; judge the fatherless ; plead for the widow."

Isa. lviii. 9. " *Is* not this the fast that I have chosen ? To loose the bands of wickedness, to undo the heavy burdens, and to let the oppressed go free, and that ye break every yoke ?"

This commands the release of all the oppressed ; and the expression "let the oppressed go free," clearly forbids involuntary
servitude, and commands the freedom of every
slave in the land.

Prov. iii. 31. "Envy thou not the oppressor, and choose none of his ways."

This clearly forbids oppression in all its
practical aspects.

Prov. xiv. 31. He that oppresseth the
poor reproacheth his maker : but he that
honoreth him hath mercy on the poor."

All slaveholders oppress the poor, and of
course reproach their maker.

Prov. xxii. 22. "Rob not the poor because
he *is* poor ; neither oppress the afflicted in
the gate."

The afflicted are oppressed in the gates of
every slaveholding city in this nation.

Jer. vii. 5—7. "For if ye thoroughly
amend your ways and your doings ; if ye
thoroughly execute judgement between a
a man and his neighbor ; If ye oppress not
the stranger, the fatherless, and the widow,
and shed not innocent blood in this place,
neither walk after other gods to your hurt :
then will I cause you to dwell in this place,
in the land that I gave to your fathers, for
ever and ever."

Jer. xxi. 12. "O house of David, thus saith
the Lord ; execute judgment in the morning,
and deliver *him that is* spoiled out of the
hand of the oppressor, lest my fury go out
like fire, and burn that none can quench *it*,
because of the evil of your doings. Behold.
I *am* against thee, O. inhabitant of the val-

ley, *and* rock of the plain saith the Lord ;
which say, who shall come down against us ?
or, who shall enter into our habitations ?"

Eccle. iv. 1. "So I returned, and considered all the oppressions that are done under
the sun : and, behold, the tears of *such as
were* oppressed, and they had no comforter ;
and on the side of their oppressors *there was*
power ; but they had no comforter."

Had the inspired writer had his prophetic
eye on the scenes of our own slaveholding
land, listening to, and beholding the groans
and sighs and tears, and wrongs of the sugar plantations, and the rice swamps, he
would not have drawn a truer picture of
those sorrow burdened and blood stained
fields.

Eccle. vii. 7. "Surely oppression maketh
a wise man mad."

Ezek. xxii. 7. In thee have they set light
by father and mother ; in the midst of thee
have they dealt by oppression with the
stranger ; in thee have they vexed the fatherless and the widow."

Every word of this is true of slavery.

Verse 29. "The people of the land have
used oppression, and exercised robbery, and
have vexed the poor and needy ; yea, they
have oppressed the stranger wrongfully."

Zeph. iii. 1. "Wo to her that is filthy and
polluted, to the oppressing city !

This is applicable to any and every slaveholding city.

Mal. iii. 5. "And I will come near to you
to judgment ; and I will be a swift witness
against the sorcerers, and against the adul

terers, and against false swearers, and
against those that oppress the hireling in *his*
wages, the widow, and the fatherless, and that
turn aside the stranger *from his right*, and
fear not me, saith the Lord of hosts."

If a man were to stand up in any of the
slaveholding cities or towns in the southern
states, and proclaim the above as a communication from himself, and as expressive of
his views of the manner in which God will
deal with the people, he would be understood to speak of slavery, and he arrested
for the same. How clear is it then that
the text comprehends slavery and denounces
it.

Only a part of the texts have been quoted
above which relate to the subject, but they
are sufficient to prove that slavery is com-
prehended in the sin of oppression, and that
it is classed with the worst of crimes. Here
the direct argument in proof of the sinful-
ness of slavery closes, and if it is not a sin
against God and man, it must be difficult to
find sin developed in human society, for it
embraces the essential elements of every possible crime. It is known that some persons
have claimed that the scriptures justify and
support slavery, but a refutation of this position, by a thorough examination of those
texts which are attempted to be pressed in
to the service of slavery, must be left
for a separate treatise.

SECTION II.

It has been proved in a series of arguments that the Bible condemns slavery ; yet some may contend that other portions of the sacred volume justify the principle of slavery, and tolerate the practice of slaveholding. This cannot be true ; if any portion of the Bible, really condemns slavery, no other portion can justify it, without an obvious self-impeachment of the record. No doubt, most persons, on a candid perusal of the arguments in support of the position that the Bible condemns slavery, will judge them of sufficient strength in themselves to settle the question, and warrant the conclusion that no part of the Bible can justify slavery ; yet as some who profess to believe the scriptures, contend for slavery, *juro divino*, and as others who may never be able to believe slavery right, may be confused and perplexed by pro-slavery assumptions and glosses, is it deemed proper to attempt an examination of those portions of the Bible which have been considered the strong hold of slavery, and see if the monster sin cannot be driven from within the lids of the sacred volume.

This undertaking is of more importance

than may be supposed by some, at first sight,
for so long as there is a lingering suspicion
that slavery finds any shelter in the Bible,
the public conscience can never be roused fully to feel its enormity.   Notwithstanding,
there may be much infidelity and scepticism
in the land, it is a fact that the Bible is generally felt to be the standard, by which the
right or wrong of human conduct must be
tested.   The almost universal circulation of
the Scriptures, the fact that all the truly
religious and prayful hold them to be given
by inspiration of God, and the manner in
which they are appealed to by all successful
debaters in our legislative halls, and by advocates in our courts of justice, proves how
strong a hold they have upon the public confidence.   It is true, there are a few persons
who openly repudiate the Scriptures, and
represent them as teaching almost every
wicked and corrupt thing, and slavery among
the rest, not to justify slavery, but to condemn the Bible.   The writer has met with a
few persons, who contended that the Bible is
a pro-slavery book, as a means of rendering
the Scriptures contemptible.   But such are
very few, and frequent developements have
proved that men who profess to disbelieve
the Scriptures, and who treat them with con-
tempt, often do it in violation of their own
convictions of right.   While they rail against
the Bible, hey thave an internal and often
illy suppressed conviction, that it is the word
of God, and that they must be judged by it.
It appears safe to conclude, that even the
infidel feels more at case in the practice of

slavery, while he is made to believe that the Scriptures justify his conduct, than when he is convinced that the Bible is against him. How important is it then, to examine the subject, and cut slavery off from all claim to support from the sacred volume? If this can be done, if it can be made to appear that no part of the Scriptures contains any warrent for human bondage in the shape of American slavery, and if this conviction can be made to take hold of the public mind, and especially the religious portion, slavery must die. Let it be felt that nothing like slavery was tolerated by the law of Moses, and let all be made to feel that there is nothing in the teachings of Jesus Christ to justify slavery, that slave catchers are not following the example of St. Paul, and that no example of slave-holding can be traced out in the history of the Apostolic Church, and all who mean to be Christians, will not only abandon it, but oppose it as they oppose any other sin. There is too much light, and too great a love of consistency, for any class of men, long to justify the practice of slaveholding, after they are constrained to admit that it is a crime against God. The conclusion is so deniable that if men may practice one great sin, they may practice any and every great sin, as interest or inclination may dictate, that but few if any will occupy the position who admit that there is a difference between right and wrong. It is only necessary then to drive slavery from the Bible, expel it from the pulpit, and chase it from the altars of religion, and it will find but little quarter in the world.

3

The Bible does not and cannot be made to justify slavery in practice, even if the principle of slavery be found in it, for want of a specific rule to govern the application of the principle in reducing it to practice. If the Bible justifies slavery, it must be as a general principle, without restriction in regard to the persons or classes to whom pertains the rights of slavery, on one hand, and the obligations of slavery on the other; or it must be in view of some specific rule which defines who shall be the master and who shall be the slave. If the Bible does not justify slavery in one or the other of these aspects, it does not and cannot justify it in any sense   On the first of these positions but little need be said.   But few if any will contend that slavery is right as a general principle, without reference to race, class, condition or distinction of persons, who possess the right to hold slaves, and upon whom rests the obligation to submit to slavery.   If slavery be right, as a general principle, in the absence of a specific rule, defining who shall be the master and who shall be the slave, every man must be at liberty to enslave whom he can.   To insist that slavery is right in the absence of any specific divine law, which clearly defines who shall be the master and who shall be the slave, is to say that the right to hold slaves is inherent in all men, and that each man is at liberty to exercise the right whenever he finds himself in possession of the power to seize upon, hold and control his fellow being.   It is also to say that the obligation to submit to be a slave, pertains equally to all men, and that each is bound to respond to it the moment a hand is laid upon him sufficiently strong to hold him. If this be so, a man can have a right to liberty only so long as he possesses sufficient power to maintain it against all aggression. This makes right depend upon might. For a man to contend that slavery is or can be right upon such a principle, is to say that it would be right to make him a slave, if a party could be found, possessing the requisite power. But the third is too absurd to need a reputation. All acts and conditions are determined to be right or wrong by some rule or law, which relates to the subject. In this case the Bible is that rule or law for the question is, does the Bible justify slavery ? The rule must then be produced from the Bible, and it must be so clear and specific as to determine who shall be the slave and who the master. Suppose the Bible said, one man may hold his fellow man as a slave ; one man can acquire the right of property in his fellow-man ; it could not justify slaveholding in any given case, unless it should at the same time point out the person who might hold slaves, and the persons whom he might hold. A man, with his Bible in one hand, lays his other hand upon his fellow, and says, you are my slave. Not so fast, says the other ; where is your authority for claiming me as a slave? The first opening his Bible reads the text which affirms that man can hold property in man, supposing there were such a text. The other replies, the law does not name you sir, as the

man owner. nor me as the man owned ; if it
justifies slave owning and holding, it will as
clearly justify me in owning and holding you,
as it will you in holding me. There is no
way to settle the dispute but by the law of
force, the stranger will prove himself to be
the slaveholder.

There can then be no sanction of slavery
found in the Bible, in the absence of a specific rule, defining clearly and certainly who
shall be the master and who shall be the
slave, and appropriating to one his rights,
and to the other his obligations. Now, it is
denied that any such rule exists, and it is believed that no sane mind will attempt to
point out such a rule upon the sacred page.
It is proposed to examine the several texts
supposed to support slavery, in which examination, two points will be kept distinctly in
view ; first none of the texts furnish the
above rule ; and, secondly, they do not even
sanction the principle of American slavery.

I. The curse that was pronounced upon
Canaan is the oldest bill of rights slaveholders are wont to plead.

" Cursed be Canaan ; a servant of servants
shall he be unto his brethren. Blessed be
the Lord God of Shem, and Canaan shall be
his servant." *Gen. ix.* 25. 26.

If I had not heard Rev. Divines quote
the above curse pronounced upon Canaan,
in support of slavery, I should never have
thought of replying to arguments founded
upon it. As it is, I reply as follows :—

1. The colored race which are the victims
of slavery in this country, are not the des-

cendants of cursed Canaan. It must be admitted by all, that the curse did not fall
upon Canaan in his own person, but that it
was prophetic of the condition of his de-
cendants of Canaan, and on them alone ; if,
therefore, the colored race are not the descendants of Canaan, it cannot justify their
enslavement. The colored race have descended from Ham, through Cush, and not through
Canaan.   The name, Ham, signifies heat,
hot, brown ; and the name, Cush, signifies
black ; while Canaan, signifies a merchant,
or trader.   When it is considered that
Hebrew names were descriptive of actions,
quality or character, and that they were often prophetically given, there is force in
these names as above defined.

It is further proved that the Colored race
are not the descendants of cursed Canaan,
by the only history we have of the family of
Noah.   The descendants of Canaan first settled the following countries, as is recorded,
Genesis x. 15–19.

"And Canaan begat Sidon his first born,
and Heth, and the Jebusite, and the Amon-
ite, and the Girgasite, and the Hivite, and
the Arkite, and the Sinite, and the Arvadite,
and the Zemarite, and the Hamathite ; and
afterward were the families of the Canaanites, spread abroad. And the border of the
Canaanites was from Sidon, as thou comest
to Gerar unto Gaza ; as thou goest unto So-
dom and Gomorrah, and Admah, and Zeboim,
even unto Lasha."

This clearly points out the nations that
were dispossessed by the Israelites, when

they came out of Egypt and took possession
of the Land of Canaan ; and in this trans·
action was fulfilled the curse pronounced
upon Canaan. The curse pronounced upon
Canaan, and the blessing pronounced upon
Shem, were prophetic. "Blessed be the
Lord God of Shem, and Canaan, shall be his
servant." The Israelites descended from
Shem, and the Canaanites, embracing the
several nations named as the Girgasites, the
Hivites, &c., descended from Canaan, and
when the Israelites came out of Egypt, they
drove out the Canaanites, destroyed some of
them and made servants of others, and they
possessed their land, and thus was this prophetic curse accomplished. How plain is all
this, and how forced and unreasonable must
be the construction which makes it a justification for American slavery.

The Cushites, the other branch of Ham's
family, from whom descended the colored
race, settled another section of the country.
Like the Canaanites, they were a seafaring
people, and sooner arrived at civilization
than did the other branches of Noah's family.
The first great empires of Assyria and
Egypt were founded by them, as were also
the republics of Sidon, Tyre and Carthage.
Our colored race are the descendants of the
people who founded and sustained those ear-
ly empires and republics. But the point in
this argument is, the race now in slavery, are
not the descendants of Canaan, upon whom
the curse of servitude was pronounced, and,
of course, that curse is no justification of
slavery as now existing.

2. The present slaveholding race are not
the descendants of Shem, to whom was ap-
propriated the service of Canaan. ".Canaan
shall be his servant;" not the servant of
some other race. If the text authorizes any
thing, it authorizes the descendants of Shem
to use the service of the descendants of Canaan ; it does not authorize any other race
to enslave them ; nor does it authorize the
Canaanites to enslave each other. Who
then are the present race of slaveholders?
Are the Shemites? It cannot be proved.
The Jews and the Arabs or Ishmaelites, are
the only people on the face of the earth who
can, with any certainty claim to have descended from Shem. The slaveholders of this
country are more likely to be the descendants of poor Canaan who was cursed. The
Canaanites were not all destroyed by the
Israelites ; indeed they left many nations un-
subdued, and were mingled with them and
were corrupted by them. Repeated and
bloody wars raged between them for many
centuries. Where are the descendants of
these nations now? I answer as follows :—
These people called Cannaanites in the
Scriptures, are known in history by the name
of Phœnicians, and it is said of them that
they began to colonize in the time of the
Hebrew Judges, and their first settlements
were Cyprus and Rhodes; thence they
pushed into Greece, Sicily, Sardinia and
Spain. *See Taylor's History.* It is then
probable that the Anglo-Saxon race came
originally from the Canaanites or Phœnicians of profane history, and these are the

people upon whom the curse was pronounced.

This presents slaveholders as taking advantage of a curse pronounced upon themselves, as a justification for enslaving another race.

3. Wave the facts set forth above, and admit that the curse imposes slavery, and that it involves the colored race, and still consequences will follow sufficient to overthrow the whole argument built upon it in support of American slavery.

(1.) In such case it would justify enslaving the whole race. If the argument proves it right to enslave any part of the race, it proves it right to enslave the whole. It would be right, therefore, to enslave every free colored person in this land, and in every other land ; it must be right to plunder Africa of all her sons and daughters until the last descendant of Ham is chattelized.

(2.) It must follow that this nation is fighting against God, and legislating against the fulfilment of divine prophecy.

If the whole race were devoted to perpetual slavery by a judicial act of Jehovah,— and the whole were thus devoted if any were, —why does this nation find fault by declaring that it is piracy upon the high seas to fulfil that supposed judicial decree of Jehovah. She has done it in a law of Congress, which declares that to bring a slave from Africa shall be judged piracy and punished by death.

Has this nation conspired with England to defeat the decrees of God, punishing with

death those who do what he has made it
right for them to do?

(3.) The argument, if allowed, would not
justify American slavery, as it is not now
confined to the colored race; there are mixed
and white slaves. The argument would justify the enslavement of none but the descendants of Canaan, if they were the colored
race, which is not the fact.

But whose descendants are the mixed
breed? One third of all the slaves in this
country have Anglo-Saxon blood in their
veins, and many of them are as white as the
fairest of the white. Others have descended
from Indians. Are these the children of
Canaan upon the assumptions of the arguments; And does the curse pronounced
upon Canaan include their enslavement?

(4.) This view of the subject, if allowed,
would subvert all the support for slavery,
attempted to be derived from the New Testament. The New Testament argument rests
upon the assumed fact that slavery exis'ed
where Jesus Christ and his apostles preached
and founded Christian churches, and that it
was not condemned by them, but that persons were allowed to hold their slaves after
being converted and received into the church.
The reply to all this is, that if slavery existed where those churches were planted, to
whom the epistles were addressed, it was not
the slavery of the colored race. If then
slavery was sanctioned by the apostles, it
was not the slavery of the African race, for
that did not then exist, and consequently,
their sanction was not based upon the curse
*2

pronounced upon Canaan. If slavery be right independently of the curse pronounced upon Canaan, as must be the case if the apostles sanctioned the slavery of their time and place, the right of it must depend upon something besides that curse, and to contend that slavery is right independently of the curse pronounced upon Canaan, is to abandon that as a ground on which to justify human bondage.

4. It was not American slavery nor yet any thing like it, that the posterity of Canaan was subjected to by the curse pronounced upon a hapless father. The curse was political subjection, political servitude, and not chattel slavery. It was shown under the first division of this argument, that the prediction was fulfilled in the overthrow of the Canaanites by the Israelites, who were the Shemites when they came out ot Egypt, and none of these transactions were analagous to American slavery, nor can they be plead as a justification of the system. The Gibeonites were made hewers of wood and drawers of water, but this was not chattel slavery. It was a public service ; no Israelite owned one of them, ncr had he any personal interterest in one of them, and they were still personally free, possessing their own lands, living in their own city, occupying their own houses, and possessing their own wives and husbands, and children. See the transaction as recorded Joshua ix. 3–27. They still existed and flourished in the days of David, as may be seen by reference to 2. Sam. xxxi. 1 –6. From this last reference. it is seen that

these Gibeonites were flourishing in posses·
sion of political rights, with power to make
their own treaty with the King of the Israel·
ites. This proves that they were not the
subjects of chattel slavery after the American pattern, and it follows that the curse
pronounced upon Canaan was not such slavery.

It has now been shown, first, that the vic·
tims of American slavery are not the des·
cendants of Canaan : secondly, that the
present race of slaveholders are not the descendants of Shem, in whose favor the curse
of servitude was pronounced upon Canaan ;
thirdly, that consequences would follow, if
the above points were yielded, which would
be fatal to American slavery as it exists ;
and, fourthly, that the curse pronounced upon
Canaan, did not involve chattel slavery or
any thing analagous to it. In the face of
these points so clearly established, slavery
must seek elsewhere for a sanction, or with-
draw its claim from scriptural support.

II. The example of Abraham, and other
patriarchs, is the next resort of slaveholders
to obtain a sanction of American slavery.

In discussing this claim of the advocates
of slavery, I shall confine myself principally
to Abraham, as his case will prove decisive
for or against slavery. As to the conduct of
Laban, in selling his daughters to Jacob, and
in giving them Zilpah and Bilhah to be their
hand maids, no effort is necessary to prove
that there was nothing analagous to American slavery involved in the transactions.
If it were clearly slavery itself, it would

not prove that, or any other slavery to be morally right, since the transactions lack the endorsement of heaven. The transactions are recorded as facts transpiring in the life of Jacob, but there is no endorsement of the character or conduct of Laban, and his conduct cannot be plead as an example to be followed, or as a justification of any system or practice. The same is true of much of the historical part of the Bible.

But in the case of Abraham, the subject wears a different aspect, as he is clearly presented as a representative man, an example to be followed, and the friend of God. If it could be clearly proved that such a man was a slaveholder, it might have the appearance of an endorsement of slavery. Now what are the facts? They are as follows :—
" He had sheep and oxen, and he had asses, and men-servants, and maid-servants, and she-asses, and camels." *Gen. xii.* 16.

"And when Abraham heard that his brother was taken captive, he armed his trained servants, born in his house, three hundred and eighteen." *Gen. xiv.* 14.

"And he that is eight days old shall be circumcised among you, every man-child in your generations, he that is born in thy house, or bought with thy money of any stranger, which is not of thy seed. He that is born in thy house and he that is bought with thy money must needs be circumcised." *Gen. xvii.,* 12,–13.

"And Abimelech took sheep, and oxen, and men-servants, and women-servants, and gave them to Abraham." *Gen. xx.* 14.

We now have before us all the essential proof that Abraham was a slaveholder, for if the above texts do not prove it, it is not proved by any other circumstance that may be mentioned in his history ; as the transactions in the case of Hagar, *Gen. xvi.* 1–9 ; and in his swearing of his servant, in relation to procuring a wife for his son Isaac, *Gen. xxiv.* 1–4.

The question is can there be found in any or all of these facts, the slightest justification of American slavery ? No ; must be the decisive answer.

1. If it were clear that Abraham was a slaveholder, which is not admitted, it would be no justification of slavery any where at any time, much less of American slavery at the zenith of the nineteenth century. The argument can be conclusive in support of the right of slaveholding, only upon the supposition that every thing which Abraham did, was not only right for him at the time and in the circumstances, but also right to be followed as an example by all men, during all time, and in all circumstances. If what was right for Abraham, in his time and his circumstances, is not necessarily right for all men now, in our circumstances, the fact that Abraham held slaves, does not prove it right for us to hold slaves now. Again, if all that Abraham did was not right, the fact that he held slaves, cannot prove slaveholding right, for if he did some things which were wrong, this act of slaveholding may have been one of those wrong things ; and if he held slaves wrongfully, it cannot prove it right for us to

hold slaves. It cannot be pretended that
Abraham's slaveholding, allowing it, has any
special endorsement by heaven, and therefore it cannot be inferred that it is right, only
on the ground that every thing which he did
was right. It takes both the above points
to make the argument good, but both points
cannot be sustained. It must be admitted
that what was innocent in Abraham at his
time and in his circumstances, is not innocent
now in our circumstances ; or else that he
did what was wrong then ; and if either of
these points be admitted, allowing him to
have been a slaveholder, it cannot prove that
slaveholding is right now. The argument
must stand thus :—All that Abraham did
was right, and what was right in Abraham
is right in us in this land and at this time.
But Abraham held slaves ; and therefore it
is right for us to hold slaves now. Let this
mode of reasoning be applied to other facts
recorded in the history of the Patriarch.

Twice did Abraham practice duplicity, if
not falsehood, by saying that his wife was
his sister. *Gen. xii.* 13, a*nd xx.* 2.

Again, Abraham, at the request of his fruit-
less wife, Sarah, took Hagar a hand-maid, a
servant girl, to his bosom and bed that he
might have children by her. Was this right?
and if so, would it be right for church-mem-
bers to practice the same thing now ? If the
fact that Abraham held slaves, proves it
right to hold slaves now, the fact that he
took one of his wife's female slaves to his
bed and bosom, and had a son by her, must
prove it right for slaveholders to practice

the same economy now. I do not know that
slaveholders will object to the conclusion,
and no doubt many practice it, but the moral
sense of all the other portions of the Christian world is against it, and it cannot be allowed.

But the above is not all, for we read that
" Abraham gave all that he had to his son
Isaac. But unto the sons of the concubines
which Abraham had, Abraham gave gifts,
and sent them away from Isaac his son, while
he yet lived, eastward unto the east country." *Gen. xxv.* 5, 6. There is clear proof
that Abraham had concubines, which is not
allowable uuder the gospel, and which the
Christian church has never allowed in any
age. If then Abraham practiced what is
clearly condemned by the Gospel, it is in
vain that the slaveholders appeal to him as
an example of slaveholding, in justification
of American slavery. His example is seen
in some things to be opposed to the Gospel,
and cannot be admitted as conclusive evidence of what is right.

2. It is perfectly plain that there was
nothing in the relation subsisting between
Abraham and his servants,analagous to Amcr-
ican slavery. It has been shown that, if
slavery had existed, it would be no justification of American slavery, but it shall now
be shown that there was no slavery in the
case. Where is the proof that Abraham's
servants were chattel slaves ?

(1.) It is not found in the word *servant*,
for this is applied to all classes of laborers
and dependents. It is not necessary at this

point to resort to criticism, but only to show
how the word is used generally in the language of those times. Abaham called himself the servant of the three angels that vis-
ited him. *Gen. xviii.* 3. He could not have
designed to have expressed the idea of a
slave. " Lot called himself the servant of
the angels which led him out of the city.
Gen. xix. 1–9. Jacob called himself the Servant of Esau. *Gen. xxx.* 5. But the re-
verse of this would be true if the word servant meant slave. " And Isaac answered
and said unto Esau, behold, I have made him
thy lord, and all his brethren have I given to
him for servants." *Gen. xxvii.* 37. The
children of Esau were not given to the children of Jacob as slaves, and servant means
only inferiority or political subjection.
Pharoah is said to have made a feast to all
his servants, *Gen. xi*, 20, but it will not be
pretended that slaves are intended. Kings
do not make feasts to slaves upon their birth
days. All subjects were the servants of
their kings, and even the highest officers of
the army, were, in the language of the times,
the servants of the sovereigns ; it is plain
therefore that the fact that Abraham had
servants, does not prove that he was a slaveholder.

(2) The proof that Abraham was a slaveholder is not found in the fact that he had
servants bought with his money. In those
times all the people were the servants of
their petty kings, and persons might be transferred from one prince to another for money,
without supposing they were chattel slaves.

During the Revolutionary war, the English Government hired an army of Germans, for which they stipulated to pay a given price per head. They were as much bought with King George's money, as Abraham's servants were bought with his money, but they were not chattel slaves. Abraham possessed of such great wealth as he was, was compelled to have servants, and leading a wandering life, amid hostile nations, it was necessary that he should have servants that were truly attached to him and his interests. To secure such servants, he may have purchased captives, to make them his free attendants, which would attach them to him. This is much more rational than to suppose he could buy them as chattel slaves, and hold them against their will, in his circumstances.

(3) The proof that Abraham was a slaveholder is not found in the fact that he had servants born in his house. Abraham had no house, in our use of the word, but dwelt in a tent ar d led a wandering life. By being born in his house, is meant, born in his family or among his attendants. With attendants enough to take care of his flocks and herds, and to protect, as a guard, his person and great wealth, there must have been many servants born in his house ; that is, among his attendants and followers, but where is the proof that they were his personal property, his chattel slaves ?

(4) The proof that Abraham was a slaveholder is not found in the fact that he had men servants and maid servants given to him by Abimelech, as above quoted. Abim-

elech gave him sheep and oxen, and as Abraham probably had as many before, as he had
servants to watch over, the attendants were
transferred, and became Abraham's followers by their own consent ; and as they were
both kings, it was only a transfer of subjects
from one government to another, and not a
gift of chattel slaves. It is clear then that
there is no proof that Abraham was a slaveholder , but it shall now be shown that there
is proof upon the face of the record that he
was not a slaveholder, in anything like the
sense of American slavery.

(1) His three hundred and eighteen trained
servants which were born in his house, could
not have been slaves in the sense of American slavery. Whatever they were, their ad-
herence to Abraham must have been voluntary. They constituted his army, and a
brave army were they, under a brave leader,
when he led them to the rescue of Lot and
the other captives, and slew the armies of
four kings, and took the spoils. It is mentioned in particular on this occasion, he
armed the three hundred and eighteen trained servants " that were *born in his own house.*"
He doubtless had other attendants at this
time, but these were taken as more reliable
in the hour of danger in a foreign expedition,
than those not born in his house, who had
more recently joined him. The latter would
most naturally be left as a home guard in
the absence of the king and the principal
army. Had any of them been chattel slaves,
how easy could they have walked away ?
Would a slaveholder of the South presume

to arm three hundred slaves and lead them into Canada, to recapture prisoners and goods that had been taken away? Abraham must have pursued those kings not less than a hundred and thirty miles, through a wild country. How easily could his slaves have escaped had they been slaves held against their wills, as our American Slaves; and how unsafe would an American slaveholder feel alone in the midst of three hundred armed slaves. Again how easily could those left at home have made their escape in the absence of their master. There were no patrols then to pick them up, no blood-hounds to pursue and run them down, and no fugitive slave law to carry them back.

2. Abraham said to God, "To me thou hast given no seed : and lo, one born in my house is mine heir." Gen., xv. 3. This was before the birth of Ishmael.

Those born in his house then, could not have been slaves or they would not have been his heirs.

3. Once more, Abraham's oldest servant ruled over all that he had, and was charged with the important business of negociating with his distant kindred for a wife for his son Isaac. The business was committed to him under the solemnities of an oath. Gen. xxiv. 1—5.

Was he a slave? Have southern planters slaves that can be trusted, not only with the care of all their estates at home, but who can be sent on a foreign embassy with a train of ten horses, and with jewels of silver, and jewels of gold, and raiment, and other prec-

ious things? Gen. xxiv. 10, 53. It is perfectly ludicrous to suppose, that persons who
were trusted with such responsibilities, bore
any analogy to southern slaves.

It is believed the record has now been
purged from every vestige of Abrahamic
slavery, and it remains to look after that
said to have been established by Moses, the
great law giver under God.

II. The Jewish polity as established by
Moses, under God, is the final resort of slaveholders to find an endorsement of American
Slavery within the lids of the Old Testament.
That there is much legislation concerning
masters and servants, and that servitude, of
some sort is tolerated, modified and regula-
ted, it would be vain to deny. But ·that
American Slavery is found upon the record,
or anything analagous to it, is denied.   Before entering upon the examination of those
provisions which some suppose involve the
principle of chattel slavery, it may be well
to state a few leading general principles,
which it will be necessary to keep in view
during the entire investigation, as having a
bearing upon the whole subject, and upon the
exposition of each text in particular.

1. The system introduced by Moses, whatever it was in fact, was a great improvement
on all former times and organisms.   If there
are what may be deemed social evils in the
light of the gospel, and which the gospel corrects, they were not introduced by Moses, but
are the relic of a more barbarous state of
things, which his system did not entirely blot
out in its great work of reformation, though it

curtailed and mitigated every evil. If any such supposed evil is found, it will be seen, not to have been introduced as a new thing, but to be there by way of a modification of some previously existing evil, the severity of which is averted by legislative restraints and protections.

2. The above remark is peculiarly true and forcible in relation to servitude, as tolerated and limited and modified by the laws of Moses. The law of Moses no where introduces a system of servitude as a new thing, or new element in society, but treats of it as a thing already existing, as an evil to be restrained, and modified. It is not possible for a reflecting mind to read the provisions touching masters and servants, without seeing, lying back of those mild provisions, a more oppressive system, which it corrects, modifies and softens. Take it as it stands upon the record, and in view of the condition of the world, and even the rude state of the Israelites, at the time it was introduced, and it must be admitted to be a most benevolent system, and greatly beneficial to all servile classes. It appears to have been introduced for the exclusive protection and benefit of the servile classes, and not for the benefit of the masters. American Slavery will have to be greatly modified before even as much as this can be said in its favor.

3. When we examine more particularly into the several provisions concerning servitude, we find that every regulation concerning it, is for the protection and benefit of the servant, and not one for the benefit of the

master. Not one new right or privilege is
bestowed upon the master ; he possessed
every right, and enjoyed every privilege, before the law was given which he can claim
and exercise under it, but it throws around
him many restraints, and many protections
around the servant, and secures to him many
rights and privileges which he would not be
likely to enjoy without the law.   It is safe
therefore to say that the whole system was
designed for the benefit of the servile classes,
which leaves not a single analogy between
it and American Slavery, as the legislation
which gives it existence, is altogether for
the benefit of the master, conferring all legal
rights on the master, and taking every legal
right away from the slave, leaving the slave
without a legal existence, and entirely unknown to the law, only as a personal chattel, only as a sheep or a horse or an ox has
a legal existence and is known in law.

These remarks, if true, and they most certainly are, must of themselves settle the entire argument, and demonstrate, that no justification can be found in Jewish servitude
for American Slavery.   I might with entire
safety rest the argument on these points, but
I propose not so to do, but only ask the reader to keep them in view, to carry them along
through the investigation, for the sake of the
light they will shed on the general subject,
and the assistance they will render in coming
at a right interpretation of the several texts
to be examined.

The way is now prepared for an examination of those parts of the Mosaic code which

some suppose teach the principle, and justify the practice of American Slavery.

The method to be pursued is, first, to examine each text by itself, and then inquire into the general bearings of the whole system upon the subject of slavery.

It will not be necessary to examine every text in which the word servant occurs, but only such of each class of texts as are regarded as the strongest proofs of the existence of slavery.

The first allusion to servitude in the Jewish economy is as follows : " And the Lord said unto Moses and Aaron, This is the ordinance of the passover : There shall no stranger eat thereof : But every man's servant that is bought for money, when thou hast circumcised him, then shall he eat thereof." Exo. xii. 43–45.

This text was not designed to create or justify slavery, if slavery be implied in its language. The most that can be made of it, is that it takes for granted that there will be servants bought with money, and hired servants, without instituting, providing for, or sanctioning either system of service. It does not refer to servitude as a thing to be established by the new system, but as a thing already existing, without bestowing upon it either sanction or censure.

It does not necessarily imply the existence of slavery. The only proof that slavery existed, is found in the fact that servants were bought with money. It will not be pretended that hired servants were slaves ; we have therefore only to settle the case of servants bought with money. The assumption that servants bought with money were chattel slaves is founded upon the supposition that the language of the Jewish law is to be interpreted by our usages. Their language was not borrowed from our usages, and cannot be safely explained by them. If it were first proved that slavery existed, then it might be safe to infer that the expression, servants bought with money, refers to slaves. Such language in a statute of one of our slaveholding States, would doubtless be so construed. It being admitted that such a class as chattel slaves existed, the language might be conclusive evidence that the legislature referred to them; but the question is not to which of two admitted classes does the language refer? but was there any such class as chattel slaves? and on this question the evidence is entirely insufficient. The assumption that there was such a class, is necessary to justify such a construction of the law, and this very construction of the law, is the only proof there was such a class. This is arguing in a circle; it is assuming the main proposition to be proved, and then offering in proof of that proposition a conclusion drawn from the assumption The language, "servant bought with thy money," cannot prove that a chattel slave is meant, only upon the supposition that no person can be bought with money, without being a chattel slave, which is false upon the very face of the record. It is only necessary to show that things and persons were bought with money, without becoming subject to the incidents of property or chattle slavery, to settle the whole question so far as the meaning of buy and bought is concerned. The word buy, in scripture language, means to get, gain, acquire, obtain, possess ; and when bought with *money* is the expression, it denotes merely the means by which the thing was obtained. A few quotations will settle this qestion.

1. The Jews bought and sold their lands for money, which lands were not. and could not be permanently alienated by such sale and purchase. They might be redeemed at any time, and if not redeemed, they must revert at the Jubilee. The price was to be according to the number of years before the jubilee when lands were sold and bought, as the following text shows :

"And if thou sell aught unto thy neighbor, or buyest *aught* of thy neighbor's hand, ye shall not oppress one another :

"According to the number of years after the jubilee thou shalt buy of thy neighbor, *and* according unto the number of years of the fruits he shall sell unto thee :

"According to the multitude of years thou shalt increase the price thereof, and according to the fewness of years thou shalt diminish the price of it : for *according* to the number *of the years* of the fruits doth he sell unto thee." Levi, xxv. 14–16.

The land was sold and bought for money, and yet no title was given or obtained to it, but only a limited possession. That possession might be for one, five, or ten years or more, as the sale was distant from the time of the jubilee. In scripture language it was

buying and selling, yet in our language, it
was no sale, but a lease for a term of years.
If then land could be bought for money,
without acquiring the right of property, but
only the right of possession and increase for
a time; it follows that men could be bought
for money without acquiring in them the
right of property, but only a right to their
labor. A man gave another possession of
his land, with the right of all the increase
for a given number of years, when it must
return to him, and this is called selling and
buying it, in scripture language. So a man
agrees to serve another for a valuable consideration, paid to him in advance, and in
scripture language he is said to sell himself,
and the other is said to buy him. If land
could be bought for money, without obtaining the right of property in it, men could be
bought for money without acquiring the
right of property in them. If land could
be bought for money without subjecting it
to all the incidents and liabilities of land
bought for money under the laws of the
United States, then men could be bought for
money, without subjecting them to all the
incidents and liabilities of men bought for
money under the laws of the slave states of
this country. The conclusion is perfectly
clear that the simple fact that servants are
said to have been bought with money, does
not prove that they were chattel slaves.

2. Hebrew servants were bought with
money and it is admitted on all hands, that
they were not chattel slaves.

"If thou buy a Hebrew servant, six years

shall he serve ; and in the seventh he shall
go out free for nothing." Exo. xxi. 2.

The man is clearly bought in the sense of
Jewish law, and yet he clearly owns himself
again on the seventh year and makes his own
appropriation of himself thereafter. This
buying men, instead of proving American
slavery, would overthrow the whole system
if incorporated into the slave code. If
slaves are held by right of the Mosaic law
they should have the privileges of that law.

"If thy brother by thee be waxen poor
and be sold unto thee, thou shall not compel
him to serve as a bond servant. Levi, xxv.
39. (For the meaning of bond servant see
hereafter on verses 44–46.)

"If a sojourner or stranger wax rich by thee
and thy brother by him wax poor, and sell
himself unto the stranger and sojourner by
thee, or to the stock of the strangers family." Verse 47.

A man is here spoken of as selling himself,
but that is not now the point. Also a distinction is made between a jew thus sold,
and a bond-servant, in the 39th verse, but
that difference is not now the question, but
shall be attended to in its place. The only
point is that Jews were bought and sold under the Mosaic law, in the sense of buy and
sell in the language of that law. This the
texts above quoted clearly prove. But Jews
could not be chattel slaves, for two reasons.
First, the Jubilee set every one of them free.
"Ye shall proclaim liberty throughout the
land unto all the inhabitants thereof." Lev.
xxv. 20. "He shall be with thee, and shall

serve thee unto the year of Jubilee, and then shall he depart from thee, both he and his children with him." Verse 40–41. Secondly, every Jew had a right in the soil, and must be returned to its possession and enjoyment at the Jubilee. "In the year of this Jubilee ye shall return every man to his possession." Verse 13: " Ye shall return every man unto his possession, and ye shall return every man unto his family." Verse 10. The point is then clear that no Jew could be a chattel slave, in the sense of American slavery, for the two reasons that all were free the seventh year, or at fatherest every fiftieth year, and all at the same time were returned to a freehold estate. The argument then stands thus :—Jews were bought and sold for money ; but Jews could not be chattel slaves, after the pattern of American slavery ; and, therefore, the simple fact that servants were bought with money, does not and cannot prove the existence of chattel slavery.

3. Wives were bought for money, or in exchange for other commodities, and yet it would not be regarded as sound to argue from thence that they were chattel slaves, or the absolute property of their husbands, in our sense of property. I will open this argument with a remarkable statute on the subject.

" And if a man sell his daughter to be a maid-servant, she shall not go out as the men-servants do.

"If she please not her master, who hath betrothed her to himself, then shall he let her be redeemed : to sell her unto a strange nation he shall have no power, seeing he hath dealt deceitfully with her.

"And if he have betrothed her unto his son, he shall deal with her after the manner of daughters.

"If he take him another *wife*, her food, her raiment, and her duty of marriage, shall he not diminish.

"And if he do not these three unto her, then shall she go out free without money."— Exo. xxi, 7–11.

The comment of Dr. Adam Clarke on the text is so peculiar that I will introduce it. Of a man's selling his daughter the Dr. says, "This the Jews allowed no man to do but in extreme distress—when he had no goods, either movable or immovable left, even to the clothes on his back ; and he had this privilege only while she was *unmarriageable*. It may appear strange that such a law should have been given; but let it be remembered that this servitude could extend, at the utmost, only to *six* years ; and that it was nearly the same as in some cases of *apprenticeship* among us, where the parents *bind* the child for *seven years*, and have from the master so much per week during that period·"

Where is the wonder that such a statute should have been given, if the code, of which it is a part, contained and enforced the system of chattel slavery, after the American model ? The law must authorize the constant sale of somebodies daughters, not for six years, but life long, to contain anything like American slavery, and it is no wonder to me, that a man should be authorized to sell his own daughters, rather than another man s daughters: I am not sure that the Dr. is right in saying that the sale was only for six years. He no doubt grounds this upon the second verse which concerns men servants, but it is said, of the daughter sold as above, she shall not go out as the men servants do, which was at the end of the sixth year.

As to what Dr. Clarke says of its being like an apprenticeship, if the remark was made of bought servants in general, I have no doubt it would be much nearer the truth, than to suppose it was like American slavery. But I believe he has entirely mistaken the design and spirit of the statute regulating the sale of daughters, as above, and will now state my own humble opinion of the text. I believe the sale of daughters named in the text, was exclusively for wives. It is true the language is, " If a man sell his daughter to be a *maid-servant*, but she was no doubt at the same time sold as a prospective wife of the purchaser or his son. According to Dr. Clarke, the sale was allowed only while the daughter was unmarriageable, and only in case of extreme poverty. Of course such sales would take place only among the poorest of the laboring classes ; and such purchases would be made, as a general rule, only by the laboring classes, as the rich would seek wives for themselves and sons among the rich. As the daughter sold belonged to the laboring class, and was sold to a purchaser of the laboring class, she must be expected to labor both before and after the sale. She is then sold as a maid-servant, but is sold at the same time as the prospective wife of the man who buys her, or of his son. She is an apprenticed wife on trial, and hence the oppression, " if she please not her master who hath betrothed her." He buys her unmarriageable, and she serves a few years and becomes a woman, and he finds she will not answer for a wife, and the design of the law is to provide for just this case. He has not yet married her, or the case would fall under the law of divorce. There are two cases provided for as follows :

(1.) "If she please not her master who hath betrothed her to himself," that is the purchaser, a provision is made to protect her. The manner in which this is introduced in connection with the sale, without explanation, proves that, in the eye of the law, to purchase, was to betroth. It is taken for granted that he who has purchased a female under that law, had betrothed her. To betroth is to contract, in order to a future marriage. If after he has thus purchased, thus betrothed, she please him not, if he find that she will not make him such a wife as he thinks he needs, he shall let her be redeemed; that is, her father may buy her back, or any of his friends that may desire her, may redeem her by paying what he gave for her, after deducting a fair proportion for what she may have earned as a servant. He shall, have no right to sell her to a strange nation, but only to take the price he paid for her a a redemption by her friends.

(2.) In case she had been betrothed to his son, and the son did not like her, when she became marriageable, the law provides for her protection. The father is held responsible to treat her as a daughter, and the son to discharge to her all the duties of a husband, and if this is not attended to, she shall go out free without money. That is, the purchaser shall not be entitled to receive back the money he paid for her, but she shall be free without being redeemed.

Here then is provision for selling persons without making chattel slaves of them. They were bought with money, without being chattels personal, as are the slaves of this country, and therefore the fact of selling and buying under the Mosaic law, does not prove that slavery existed under that law. But the object of quoting the above text has been to prove that wives were bought, and this it proves beyond doubt. That I have not mistaken the law, in supposing the sale was a betrothing of the female sold, is clear from the fact that in other cases female servants went out at the end of the sixth year, as is seen from Exo. xv. 12–17. From these references it is clear that according to the general law, female servants were released at the end of the sixth year, but in the case under consideration, it is said they shall not go out as the men servants do; in the place of this another provision is made, founded upon the ground that they are betrothed.

But there is other proof that wives were bought. Jacob bought both his wives of Laban their father. Gen. xxix. 18–27.

David purchased Michael, Saul's daughter to be his wife. 1 Sam. xviii. 27. Shechen son of Hamor the Hivite, wished to purchase Dinah, Jacob's daughter for a wife, and offered any price they should demand. Gen. xxxiv. 11–12. Hosea bought a wife an paid for her, part in silver and the balance in barley. Hosea. iii. 2. Boaz said, "Ruth the Moabites have I purchased to be my wife." Ruth, iv. 10. The word *purchased*, is rendered *bought* in the margin.

Enough has been said to show that it was a common thing to purchase wives, that they were bought with money. The evidence that slavery existed is the fact that servants were bought with money, but wives were also bought with money from which it must follow either that the fact that servants were bought does not prove that they were slaves, or else the fact that wives were bought must prove that they were slaves. If servants were slaves because they were bought, then wives were slaves because they were bought. If wives were not chattel slaves, though bought with money, then servants were not necessarily chattel slaves because they were bought with money. If a wife could be bought with money with becoming a chattel slave, then buying with money does not constitute or prove the existence of chattel slavery, and the argument in proof that slavery existed, founded upon the fact that servants were bought with money, must fall to the ground. It must be true that servants were not slaves *because they were bought*, or else that wives were slaves *because they were bought.*

4

If the ground be taken, as a last resort to support slavery, that such wives as were bought with money, were the absolute property of their husbands, and were so regarded and treated in that rude state of society, nothing will be gained. As the object is to prove that American slavery is right, the argument can be sound only upon the ground that what was practiced and tolerated then, must be right now. If all the facts alleged were admitted, viz., that chattel slavery did exist under the Mosaic code, it would not prove American slavery right, only upon the ground that what that code allowed is now right. But that code allowed parents to sell their daughters for wives and therefore such a practice must be right now. To make any argument good, we have got to take with it, all the consequences which necessarily follow from the premises. If servants were chattel slaves because they were bought, wives were slaves because they were bought. If it is right now to buy slaves because slaves were bought under the Mosaic law, it must be right to buy wives now because wives were bought under the Mosaic law. And if it be right now to hold persons in chattle slavery because it was done under the Mosaic law, it must be right, not only to buy wives, but also to hold them as chattel slaves, because it was practiced under the Mosaic law. Some of the lords of creation may be ready to admit all these consequences, and be glad to have it so, yet the better half of humanity will be so unanimous in repudiating the doctrine, that the argument, carrying with it such consequences, cannot be sustained. If then it would now be regarded as a violation of the principles of the Gospel for parents to sell their daughters for wives, and for men to buy wives for themselves and sons to be owned as personal chattels, there is no proof in the Mosaic law, that American slavery is not a violation of the principles of the Gospel. If the one was practiced under the law, the other was; and if the one is now right, because it was practiced under the law, the other must be.

It has been showed that Hebrew servants could be held only for the period of six years. To this rule there is one exception which should be noticed as of some importance. The whole provision reads thus:

"If you buy a Hebrew servant, six years he shall serve: and in the seventh he shall go out free for nothing.

"If he came in by himself, he shall go out by himself: if he were married, then his wife shall go out with him.

"If his master have given him a wife, and she have borne him sons or daughters, the wife and her children shall be her master's and he shall go out by himself.

"And if the servant shall plainly say, I love my master, my wife, and my children; I will not go out free:

"Then his master shall bring him unto the judges: he shall also bring him to the door, or unto the door post: and his master shall bore his ear through with an awl; and he shall serve him for ever." Exo. xxi. 2–6.

On this provision I remark,

1. It was clearly instituted for the benefit and protection of the servant, and not for the master's benefit. It confers no right, no discretionary power upon the master, save the right of retaining the wife and children in a given case, but it does bestow a discretionary power upon the servant. It is this, the servant sells himself for six years, and no more—"Six years shall he serve, and in the seventh he shall go out free"—but the law gives the servant the power to extend the contract at the end of the sixth year, to, "for ever," as our translaters have rendered it, but which I suppose means unto the Jubilee. The master has no power to hold him another day, if he wishes to leave at the end of the sixth year ; he has no power to turn him away ; if the servant wishes to stay, he is compelled to retain him. Thus is it seen that the law is all on the side of the servant, and this does not look much like American slavery.

2. The provision is clearly to protect the servant against being separated from his wife and children, in the case where the master has the right of retaining them. This is in case the master has given him a wife. This wife might be the master's daughter, for which the servant may be supposed not to have paid the customary dowery. Or the wife may be a Hebrew maid servant, having one, two, three or four of the six years yet to serve before she can go out Or, what is more probable, the wife may be a servant from the Gentiles, a proselyte, bound to serve until the jubilee. In either of these cases,

it would be doing violence to the marriage
relation to send the servant away without
his wife and chileren, and hence the law provides that the servant may demand an extension of the contract of his servitude "for
ever," that is, as I understand it, to the jubilee. Let but this provision be introduced
into American slavery, and let the separation
of husbands and wives, parents and children
be thus interdicted, and it will soon destroy
the whole system. How strange it is that
what would overthrow the whole system of
slavery if introduced and enforced, should
be relied upon for its support!

3. Whatever may be thought of the law
under consideration, in all other aspects, it
is certain that the service is voluntarily entered into, on the part of the servant, after
trying it six years, and this destroys all analogy to American slavery. The proceeding
of boring the servants ear with an awl, is
merely a prescribed form of recording the
testimony in such cases, and has no bearing
on the main point at issue. I will not crit-
icise upon the words "for ever," which I suppose means until the jubilee, as this will
come up for consideration hereafter in connection with another text.

The next resort of slavery is to the following provision of the law.

"If a man smite his servant or his maid,
with a rod, and he die under his hand; he
shall surely be punished. Nothwithstand-
ing, if he continue a day or two, he shall not
be punished "for he is his money." Exo. xxi.
20-21.

This law does not institute or establish slavery, or any kind of servitude. It merely refers to it, for the purpose of settling a rule of jurisprudence, applicable in peculiar cases. It assumes the fact that there are masters and servants, but it does not establish, legalize or justify the relation, but it provides for the administration of justice between the parties in a given case. The only proof which the text can be supposed to furnish in support of slavery, must depend upon two circumstances. The fact that the master presumes to smite the servant with a rod, and the fact that the servant is declared to be the master's *money*. These two points need examination.

Does the fact that the law presumes that a master may smite his servant with a rod that he die, prove that the servant is a chattel slave? Surely not. There is no proof that the smiting is in any sense authorized or justified by this or any other law. Smiting itself is not justified, even if it be not unto death. The laws of our slaveholding states authorize masters directly to punish their slaves, but no such liberty is given in the Scriptures. We challenge the production of the first text which authorizes a master to inflict corporal correction upon a servant. Parents are required to correct their children. This principle is contained in all the following texts. Deut. viii. 5 ; Prov. iii. 12 ; xiii. 24 ; xix. 18 ; xxiii. 13–14 ; xxix. 15–17 ; Heb. xii. 7–9. While the scriptures are so full and explicit on the subject of the correction of children by parents, there is not one text which requires masters, or even authorizes them to punish their servants. Again, the law provides that parents, who have a son whom they cannot govern, may hand him over to the public authorities to be judged and punished, but there is no such provision for masters, who have disobedient servants. See Deut. xxi. 18–22. The punishment of servants is without lawful authority and is always unlawful. If it be supposed that the fact that it is made punishable for a master to kill his servant with a rod, renders it lawful to beat him with a rod, provided he does not kill him; the reply is, that the same mode of reasoning will prove it lawful for men to fight, provided they do not kill or disable each other. The 18th and 19th verses provide for a case where two men strive together, and one smites the other with a stone or his fist. Will it be contended that the striving is thereby rendered lawful? Certainly not. No more is it rendered lawful for a master to beat his servant with a rod, because the law provides that he shall be punished if he kills him while doing so.

The fact then that the scriptures take it for granted that a master is liable to get in a passion and smite his servant that he die, and provides for his punishment, does not give the least countenance to slavery.

But "he is his money." This doubtless is regarded as the strong hold of slavery. All that is necessary for me to prove is that it does not necessarily involve chattel slavery, and this will be easily accomplished.

1. The statute is a general one, including all classes of servants, many of whom, it has been seen, were not and could not be chattel slaves. The 26th and 29th verses are of the same general character. If a man smote out the eye or the tooth of a servant, he was free. These laws protect all kinds of servants, Hebrew servants as well as others. It has been shown that Hebrew servants were bought with money, and of course, it was just as true of these that they were the money of their masters as of others. As the text affirms of a Hebrew servant as clearly as of any other, "he is his money," and as a Hebrew servant could not be a chattel slave, the text affirms that he is money who cannot be a slave, and therefore it cannot prove those to be slaves of whom it affirms.

2. the language is most clearly figurative, and can be literally true only in a sense which divests it of all proof of chattleship.

"He is his money." All money in those days was gold or silver. But the servant was neither gold or silver, and was not money. A literal translation would strengthen this view. The expression, "he is his money" literally translated would read, "his silver is he." But a servant is not silver, is not money, but flesh and blood and bones, body and soul. What then is meant by the expression? Simply this, he has cost the master money, the master has the value of money in him, and loses money's value by his death. But this is true of all servants bought with money, or whose wages are paid in advance, and therefore the expression

cannot prove that the servant said to be
money is a chattel slave.

3. The obvious intention of the whole
statute, as well as of that particular clause,
requires no such construction, but the end is
reached just as clearly and forcibly without
involving the chattel principle.

The design of the general statute is to secure the condemnation of the master in case
of wilful murder, and thereby furnish greater
security to the servant ; as well as to secure
the master against being put to death as a
murderer, when no murder was intended.

It is not to be inferred that the killing is
to be punished as inferior crime, because the
killed is a servant. The translation perverts
the sense. The word, *nakam* translated
punished, should be rendered *avenged*. It is
not the master that is to be avenged, but the
servants death, which, under the circumstances necessarily means that the master shall
be put to death as a murderer. This word,
though it occurs repeatedly in the Old Testament, is translated punished in no other text,
but is generally translated avenged and in a
very few instances, to take vengence or to
revenge. The word is thus defined in Roy's
Hebrew and English Dictionary : " *Nakam*.
1. He recompensed or paid ; 2. avenged,
revenged, cut off, as murderers ; 3. vindicated, advocated, as the cause of another."
The object of the statute is to secure such
execution in one case, and to prevent it in
another.

If the master smite his servant with a rod,
and he die under his hand, the death shall

surely be avenged.   The instrument is a rod,
not an axe.   A man might kill with an axe,
without intending it, but not with a rod.   If
the servant died under his hand, and a rod
only was used, the proof is positive that he
meant to kill him, and must have done it
wilfully and by protracted torture.   Though
a man might be likely to take some more fatal instrument, if he meant to kill, yet the
fact that he did kill with such an instrument,
is proof positive that he meant to kill, and
the avenger is authorized to smite him as a
murderer.

But suppose the servant does not die under his hand, but continues a day or two,
then his death shall not be avenged.   And
why ?   Because the evidence is not clear
that he meant to kill him.   He did not kill
him on the spot, as he would most likely have
done had he designed to take his life.   Moreover it was only a rod with which he smote
him, and this is presumptive evidence that he
did not mean to kill him ; had he designed
his death, he would have been likely to se-
lect a more fatal instrument than a rod with
which to smite.   Finally, " he is his money ;"
that is, he has a monied interest in him, and
looses the worth of money by his death, and
this is an additional proof that he did not
mean to kill him.   The design of this statement, "he is his money," is to show that the
master's monied interest was againt his killing the servant, that he lost money by his
death, and this is just as clear in the case of
a Hebrew servant bought with money, who
could not be a chattel slave.   The monied

argument is good in the case of any servant,
whose wages is paid in advance, and as that
kind of service was common, the idea of
chattel slavery is not in the least involved.
It is no part of the design of the text to
create, legalize or justify the right of property in man, but merely to use the fact of a
monied interest in a man, as collateral evidence that murder was not intended, and
this object is secured as well without the
assumption of chattel slavery as it is by re-
sorting to that terrible position. It need
only to be remarked that the law in question
provides only for the case, as a public of-
fence. There can be no question that the
servant, in case of abuse or injury, might
appear in the court against his master, and
receive justice at the hands of the judges, in
an action for private damages.

I now approach the last resort of slavery
within the lids of the Old Testament, to
which it must be expected to cling as a man
of blood to the horns of the altar, when the
lifted arm of the avenger is seen near at hand.
The law in question reads as follows :

" Both thy bondmen, and thy bondmaids,
which thou shalt have, *shall be* of the heathen
that are round about you ; of them shall ye
buy bondmen and bondmaids.

"Moreover, of the children of the strangers
that do sojourn among you, of them shall ye
buy, and of their families that *are* with you,
which they begat in your land : and they
shall be your possession.

" And ye shall take them as an inheritance
for your children after you, to inherit *them*

for a possession ; they shall be your bondmen
forever : but over your brethren, the children of Israel, ye shall not rule one over another with rigor." Lev. xxv. 44–46.

I might grapple with slavery upon the
ground of the common translation, as above,
and beat it ; but I am not disposed so to do,
until I shall have exposed its hand in cor-
rupting the translation. I have already
made one correction in the common translation in the preceding text, and as I design to
gronnd an argument upon a new translation
of the present important text, I will explain
the whole matter at this point. I admit
there should be strong reasons for departing
from the common English version of the
Scriptures, a version generally approved and
allowed to be correct. The translators were
men of great learning, and executed their
trust with great ability and fidelity, and have
in general seized upon the very spirit and
nerve of the original, so far as it can be represented by English words ; yet believe
they were deceived by the spirit of slavery
into a false translation of the text under consideration, as perhaps in a few other texts.
The slave trade was in the hight of its progress at the time the translation took place.
It had previously attracted the attention of
Church and State. At first it met with opposition from both. The first grant of the
privilege of bringing slaves to America, was
by Charles V. in 1517. This appears to
have been principally. secured by the repre-
sentations of Las Casas a priest, and afterwards a bishop. But after this, Charles re-

pented of the countenance he gave the slave trade, and Pope Leo X., his cotemporary, denounced the system, and declared that not only the Christian religion, but nature itself cried out against a state of slavery." About the year 1556 Queen Elizabeth was deceived into a permit granted to Sir John Hawkins, to bring negros from Africa; and she charged him not to carry them to America without their consent. But these scruples were overcome by the false glosses put upon this and other texts by interested priests, and by the great profit of the traffic. Here the matter rested, and all took it for granted without further examination, that these pro-slavery expositions were right, and when King Jame's translators commenced their work in 1607, they very naturally adopted the false expositions designed to countenance the slave trade, and translated the text under consideration, as well as some others, in the light of those false glosses by which they avoided coming in contact with the slave trade, then in its greatest prosperity in England.

I will now notice the translation itself. The principal errors are as follows: There is nothing in the original to justify the words "*bond-men and bond-maids;*" it should be man-servant and woman-servant. Both are in the singular, and not plural, in the Hebrew text. The word translated *buy* is most properly translated *procure*. The word translated *heathen*, is properly rendered *Gentiles*, and might be rendered nations. The word translated *forever* cannot bear that rendering in this case; it cannot mean longer than

natural life, and that is never the sense of
the English word *forever*. The word rendered *forever*, is *le-o-lam*, and its proper meaning is endless, and is correctly rendered *forever*, or *to eternity*, but here it cannot be understood in its full sense. It is used to denote a long period, less even than the whole
of time. Many rites of the Jews were to be
observed *forever*, which forever has past and
ended. A single text will serve as an illustration of the use of the word in a limited
sense. " Bath-shbea said Let my lord king
David live forever." 1 Kings i. 31.

This can mean but a short indefinite period,
for David was then old. It can mean no
more than a long time, for a man in his circumstances. But in the expression, " they
shall be your bond-men forever," forever can
mean no more than natural life, and yet it is
never employed to express this indefinite
period. Forever, therefore, does not express
the sense of the text, and as the period of the
jubilee was the longest time a person could
be retained in service by one contract, which
will hereafter be more fully shown, it is certain that forever could not extend beyond
the jubilee, and it is most natural to understand it as refering to that period, or to some
period to be fixed upon in the contract, but
not named in the law. I will now introduce
a literal translation of the text, and as I have
no reputation as a Hebrew scholar to sustain
one of my own. I have written to Dr. Roy,
author of Roy's Hebrew and English Dictionary, for a literal translation of the text
under consideration, and he has kindly fur-

nished me with the following, which he warrants to be correct and literal.

44. "And thy man servant, and thy woman servant, shall be to thee from among the Gentiles which are round about you. From them ye shall procure a man servant and a woman servant.

45. "And also of the children of Foreigners that reside with you, from them ye may procure of their families which are with them, that were born in your land; they shall be to you for a possession. (service.)

46. "And ye shall choose them for your children after you, to preside over them as their portion, unto the end of the time (specified)."—*Roy.*

I think no Hebrew scholar will deny that this translation is correct in all essential particulars, and if it be so, it follows, not only that the translation in the common version perverts the sense of the original text to support slavery, but that nothing like American slavery is found in the law of Moses, when it is correctly understood. Take the text as it is now spread before the reader, and there is clearly no slavery in it; no human chattels are presented to the mind, no fettered limbs are seen, and no chains clank in the ear of humanity. It is certain that the text as rendered above, does not and cannot prove the existence of chattel slavery; but still it means something, and what does it mean? This is an important inquiry. Every law should be considered as designed to secure some important end, especially when God is the Legislator. This law cannot have been

designed to establish a system of human bondage like American slavery, and must have
been designed to secure some other end, and
not only a benevolent end, but one consonant
with the general design of the whole system
of which it is a part. It will give additional
strength to the conclusion, that the establish-
ment of slavery was not its object, if it can
be clearly shown that it was designed and
calculated to secure another benevolent and
important end. This I will now attempt to
show. I regard the law in question, in a
civil point of light, as prescribing a plan of
naturalization for foreigners ; and in a religious point of light, as a system of proselytism, by which heathen were to be reclaimed
from their idolatry, to the faith and worship
of the God of Abraham. To show this a
number of plain facts need to be collected
and looked at in connection with each other,
and with reference to their joint bearing on
this question.

1. God designed to make of the Jews a
numerous, wealthy and powerful nation. To
secure this they must occupy a productive
country, which he gave them, described as
" a land flowing with milk and honey." It
was necessary also that they should be kept
from being mingled with other nations, either
by emigration to other countries, or by a
large influx of strangers, who should not become identified with their religion and
nationality. It was necessary to keep them
a distinct people. Further to secure this end,
their lands were secured forever, beyond
their power to alienate them, so that every

Jew was a freeholder in fact, or in prospect.
A foreigner could not become permanently
possessed of their lands, and could obtain a
lasting interest in them only by becoming
incorporated with some branch of the Jewish
family, for which proivsion was made. This
separating and signalizing the Jews had reference to the execution of God's plan of re-
deeming mankind, for which it was a preparatory step. So far all is plain and will not
be disputed.

2. The proposed position of the Jewish
nation, with the means employed to secure it,
the inalienability of their lands, tended to
produce certain incidental evils, and a want
of an element essential to the greatness and
independence of any people, viz. a numerous
and well sustained laboring class, beyond
the actual proprietors of the soil. A freehold interest, is the greatest interest, and the
cultivation of the soil is and ever must be
the basis of all other great interests, yet
there are other great interests that must be
sustained. The circumstances of the Jews
tended to produce a want of such a laboring
class. A few of the influences tending to
produce this want shall be named.

(1.) They were all land owners, and none
need therefore engage in other pursuits than
cultivating the soil, unless reduced by misfor-
tune or bad economy. This would produce
but very few mechanics, and laborers to be
hired.

(2.) Such was the richness of their country,
so great the productiveness of the soil, that
a large amount of labor could be expended
5

with profit to the land owner, while the fact
that every one was a land owner, tended to
render such labor difficult to obtain. In
every prosperous community there is needed
many more laborers than actual land owners,
some must operate as mechanics, some as mer-
chants, some must cultivate the lands of the
unhealthy and widows, some must labor as additional helps to those who cultivate their
own lands, and others will be needed as
domestic help, commonly called servants.

(3.) The religion of the Jews required them
to devote a large portion of their time to its
special duties and exercises, rendering more
laborers necessary to accomplish the same
amount of labor in a given season. Every
seventh year was a Sabbath the whole year.
This was one seventh of all the time, and if
averaged among the seven years, would be to
each year just equal to the weekly Sabbath.
For proof of this seventh year rest, see Lev.
xxv. 3–7. Next was the weekly Sabbath,
every seventh day. Exo. xx. 8–11. This
was another seventh of their whole time.
Then there were three annual feasts; the
Passover, which lasted seven days; the Pen-
tecost or feast of weeks, which lasted seven
days; and the feast of Tabernacles, which
lasted eight days. For proof of these feasts
see Deut. xvi. 3, 10, 16; Exo. xii. 3, 6, 15;
Lev. xxiii. 35, 36, 39, 41, 42, See also Jose-
phus, Book III. Ch. X.

Their national feasts were held in one
place, the place which the Lord chose, which
was Jerusalem, and thither the tribes went
up to worship. Exo. xxiv. 23; Deut. xvi.

16 ; Luke ii. 41, 44. This required long
journies on the part of many, as Joseph and
Mary went one whole day's journey home-
ward, before they missed their remarkable
son, so large was the company returning from
the feast.   More time must have been spent
in the necessary preparations and journey,
than in the feasts themselves.   The feasts
together occupied twenty-two days, which
gives the following result.   The seventh year
rest is equal to one weekly Sabbath, or fifty-
two days in a year.   To this add the weekly
Sabbath, fifty-two days per year more, making one hundred and four days.   To this add
the three annual feasts, together occupying
twenty-two days, making a total of one hundred and twenty-six, which is five days more
than one entire third of the year occupied in
religion. To this might be added the time consumed in going and returning, as above supposed, and other feasts that might be pointed
out, as every new moon, and special occasions
by which it would appear that one half or
more of the time of the whole male population was occupied with religious matters, but
it is not necessary to press these additional
matters, as it would cumber my page with
many references to establish the several
points. I have shown positively that over
one third part of their time was occupied by
religious matters, and that is sufficient for
my argument. This must have required an
increased number of laborers.   It should be
remarked that all that class of servants which
some suppose to have been slaves, were required to observe all these feasts, and

Sabbaths. It may be asked how it could be expected that they should become great and wealthy, with a religion laying so heavy a tax upon their time. The answer is plain, in the words of the Law Giver himself. " And if ye shall say, What shall we eat the seventh year ? behold we shall not sow nor gather our increase : then I will command my blessing upon you in the sixth year, and it shall bring forth fruit for three years." Lev. xxv. 20, 21. While they obeyed God, the shadow of his wing protected and blessed their whole land, but when they sinned and lost the divine blessing, without an abatement of their religious taxes, they felt them to be a burden. The system was not adapted to the whole world, embracing all countries and climates : and it was established by God only as a preparatory step, to last until the time of reformation, when they should pass away with what Paul calls " a yoke which neither our fathers nor we were able to bear." But while the system lasted it had to be made consistent with itself, and if one part tended to produce incidental evils, they had to be overcome by the action of some other part. One evil we have seen was a want of a sufficient number of laborers. This would naturally and mainly result first, from the inalienability of their lands, making all the Jews land owners ; secondly, from the same fact tending to prevent other people from settling among them on account of their not being able to obtain a freehold estate ; thirdly, from their religion, which consumed so much of their time ; and fourthly, from the danger

to their whole system, which would arise
from allowing laborers from other nations in
sufficient numbers to become resident among
them, without being naturalized and brought
under the controlling influence of their laws
and religion. To overcome this difficulty,
the celebrated law was introduced, now under consideration, authorizing them to obtain
servants from the Gentiles. "Thy man servant and thy woman servant shall be to thee
from among the Gentiles. From them ye
shall procure a man servant and a woman
servant." The law has two faces to it, and
removes two evils at once.

First, it renders the employment of Gentiles lawful, and thereby supplying the demand for laborers, and increases the population. Secondly, it removed a temptation
to which they would otherwise have been exposed, to oppress and degrade one another.
Some in every community will be unfortunate
or prodigal, and fall into decay, and become
dependent. This is contemplated in the law,
verses 35, 36, 39, 42. Owing to the want of
laborers and domestics, resulting as above,
the wealthy might have been tempted to keep
the poor down, for the sake of being able to
obtain their services ; but this the law pre-
vents in two ways. First, it forbids it in so
many words, and secondly, it opens another
door through which servants can be lawfully
obtained. Such servants were, by the very
operation of that law, naturalized and became
finally incorporated with the Jewish nation,
and possessed in common with them all their
civil and religious privileges and blessings.

Thus did this law, which has been so terribly perverted and abused to make it justify American Slavery, supply the land with labor, and at the same time naturalize the labor to the nation, and proselyte him to the faith and worship of the true God.

But how were these servants obtained. Our translation says they were bought. If it were so, it would be clear that they voluntarily sold themselves, and used the price as they saw fit for their own benefit. Of whom else could they be bought, by men whose law provided that "he that stealeth a man and selleth him, or if he be found in his hand shall surely be put to death." Exo. xxi. 16. There is no law in all the book of God, by any provision of which, one man can get another into his possession to sell him in the market, without stealing. The law of the Jews punished the stealing and selling of men with death, and would he buy such stolen men? The right to buy involves the right to sell, on the part of him of whom the purchase is made. There being no way by which a man can obtain possession of a man to sell him but by stealing him, they could have been bought of none but themselves. It is true they might buy captives out of the hands of the heathen, but captives are stolen if held and sold as slaves. They could therefore rightfully buy captives, only to free them, for as the captor has no title to captives, so he can sell none, and the buyer can buy none. If we understand by buying, merely engaging the services of men for a specified time for a valuable consideration agreed upon be-

tween the parties, the subject is all plain.
Then might the Gentiles sell themselves to
the Jews, or parents might sell their children
to the Jews, by which they apprenticed them
to the Jewish state as prospective citizens,
and to the Jewish religion. I know not how
Gentile parents could have done better by
their children. It presented a brighter prospect than the sale of children does now in
the human markets.

But we have seen that the word buy in our
sense of the term, is not in the text, that it
is *procure*. Well, how were they procured ?
A Jew shall testify. Dr. Roy, in sending
me the translation above given, accompanied
it with the following :

"There is no word in the Bible for *slave ;*
a ved is the only word to be found there ;
and means a hired man, servant, laborer, sol-
dier, minister, magistrate, messenger, angel,
prophet, priest, king, and Christ himself.
Isa. lii. 13; but it never means a *slave for life.*

For *the law of the Sanhedrim* forbids slavery.

"1. The contract was to be mutual and
voluntary.

"2. It was conditional that the servant
should within one year become a Proselyte
to the Jewish religion ; if not, he was to be
discharged.

"4. If he became such, he was to be gov-
erned *by the same law*, to eat at the same table, sup out of the same dish. and eat the
same Passover with his master.

"5. Finally, the law allowed him to marry
his master's daughter. Prov. xxix. 21. Yan-
kee in Sanhedrim."

This confirms the view I have given that
the law presented a system of naturalization
and of proselytism. The circumstances of
the case were such as to call for such a provision. In addition to what has been said
of the necessity of some source whence laborers might be obtained, if we look at the
condition of the Gentiles, we shall see that
their circumstances pointed them out as that
source, under proper regulations and restric-
tions. They were generally inferior to the
Jews in point of intelligence and civilization,
and on the subject of religion, they were in
the darkest midnight, while the Jews enjoyed
the light of heaven. They were divided
into petty kingdoms, and were but little
more than the servants of their kings, who
wielded an arbitrary if not an absolute scep-
ter over them. But moral advantages are
above all other advantages, and these were
found only in the land of Israel ; over that
land the wing of the Almighty was spread ;
there the Angel of the Covenant watched
behind the veil, and the divine presence
glowed upon the mercy seat above the ark,
and from that land alone, the way shown
clearly that leads to heaven. If David who
had danced before the unvailed ark, could
exclaim, "I had rather be a door keeper in
the house of my God, than to dwell in the
tents of wickedness, to bring a Gentile from
the darkness of idolatry to the tent service
of an Israelite, where God's own institutions
shown upon him must have been a transition
over which angels rejoiced. A position
which wor'd have been menial to a native

Jew, was honor, exultation and even salvation to a Gentile, coming from the land of shadows and death.

To this must be added what we must suppose was the case, that numbers of heathen were attracted by the Great fame of the Jews, that the report of what God had done for them, and of all the wonders he had wrought, and how he dwelled in that land, spread even among the surrounding nations, and that many resorted there, even to better their condition as servants. But it would not have been safe to have left these matters to regulate themselves, or to the will of each individual contracting party without the restraints of law, and hence all the laws regulating the subject of servitude.

The Jews were authorized to take the heathen that might come to them, on condition that they became proselytes to their religion and then when they were fully inducted, they became citizens with all the rights of native Jews, and their children born in the land were regarded as native Jews. There can be no doubt many became proselytes by this system, which rendered the truth and altars of God accessible to the Gentiles even under the mosaic system. And this proselyting the Gentiles was but the first fruits of their future grand gathering in Christ Jesus. And that Gentile blood was introduced into Jewish veins is evident ; for David the brightest lamp of the nation, descended on the side of his mother, from a Moabitess women, who became a proselyte to the Jewish religion.

SECTION III.

It remains to be proved that slavery finds no sanction in the New Testament, and the argument will be finished. It is a strange position which affirms that He who came to preach deliverance to the captives, and the opening of the prison-doors to them that are bound, and who gave himself a ransom for all, made provision in his system of government for leaving one portion of his people the absolute property and slaves of others, from the dark hour of life's opening sorrows, until they find a refuge in the arms of death and in the darker sleep of the grave ! But as strange as this position is, it is attempted to be maintained, and needs to be met and refuted.

Let it be understood, the present argument is not to be based upon those scriptures which are supposed to condemn slavery ; those have been urged in direct arguments previously advanced. The only point that remains to be examined is, does the New Testament teach in any text or texts, in the use of any words or form of speech, that slavery is or can be right ? As slavery is a positive institution, an arbitrary and unnatural condition, sustained by force on one hand, and in-

voluntary submission on the other, it is not
a sufficient justification to say that Christ or
his apostles did not condemn it, were that
true ; it must be proved that they authorized
it. We may demand of the slave holder, who
appropriates his fellow-beings to his own use
as chattels, "by what authority doest thou
these things, and who gave thee this authority ?" In reply to this they point us to certain texts, and words, and forms of speech
which were used by Christ and his apostles,
and tell us that they justify slavery. We
will now examine them.

It is well known that the words slave,
slaveholder, and slavery, are not found in our
English translation of the New Testament ;
and if the thing is found at all, it must be in
the original Greek, and not in the translation.
The word *slave* occurs once in the English
translation. Rev. xviii. 13 : "Slaves and
souls of men." Here the word rendered
slaves, is *soma* which literally signifies *bodies*,
and should have been translated "bodies and
souls of men."

CONSIDERATION OF THE SEVERAL TERMS USED.

In the Greek language, there are three
words which may mean a slave, *andrapodon*,
arguronetos, and *doulos*. The first of these,
andrapodon is derived from *aneer*, a man, and
pous, the foot, and signifies a slave and
nothing but a slave. If this word had been
used, it would have be n decisive, for it has
no other signification but a slave ; but this
word is found nowhere in the New Testament.

The second word, *arguronetos*, is derived from *arguros*, silver, and *oneomai* to buy, and hence it signifies to buy with silver; or a slave, doubtless, from the fact that slaves were bought with silver. This word is nowhere found in the New Testament.

The third word, is *doulos*. This word occurs more than a hundred and twenty times in the New Testament, and may mean a slave, or a free person, who voluntarily serves another, or a public officer, representing the public or civil authority. As the word occurs so frequently, it will be necessary to notice only a few instances in which it is used in its several senses. If the word properly mean *slave*, it would be true to the original to translate it *slave*, where it occurs. I will first give a few instances in which it cannot mean slave. " On my servants, [*doulos*] and on my hand-maidens [*doulee*] I will pour out in those days, of my spirit." Acts. ii. 18.

Here the word is used to denote christian men and women in general as the servants of God. It would read very strange to translate it slave; upon my *men slaves*, and upon my *female slaves* will I pour out in those days of my spirit.

" And now Lord, behold their threatenings : and grant unto thy *servants* that with all boldness they may speak thy word." Acts iv. 29. Here the word is used to denote the apostles or preachers. It would be no improvement to translate it, grant unto thy *slaves*, &c. " Paul a servant of Jesus Christ, called to be an apostle." Rom. i. 1. Would it improve it to read, Paul the *slave* of Jesus Christ?

"We preach not ourselves but Christ Jesus the Lord, and ourselves your *servants* for Jesus sake." 2 Cor. iv. 5. We preach ourselves your *slaves* for Jesus sake, would not only be without warrant, but it would make it conflict with Paul's declaration, that he was the *slave* of Jesus Christ. To be the slave of two distinct claimants at the same time is impossible.

"James a servant [*slave*] of God, and of the Lord Jesus Christ." James i. 1.

"As free, and not using your liberty for a cloak of maliciousness, but as the servants,]*slaves*] of God." 1 Peter ii. 16.

"Simon Peter a servant [*slave*] and an apostle of Jesus Christ." 2 Peter 1. i.

"Jude the servant [*slave*] of Jesus." 1.

"And he sent and signified it by his angel to his servant [*slave*] John." Rev. i. 1.

"Hurt not the earth, neither the sea, nor the trees, till we have sealed the servants [*slaves*] of our God in their foreheads," Rev. vii. 3. It is not impossible but this text may be urged in justification of the practice of slaveholders, of branding their slaves with the name of the owner.

Enough has been said to show that the word *doulos*, does not necessarily mean slave, in the sense of chattel slavery. Indeed it is only in a few instances, out of the one hundred and fifty times in which it is used, that it can be pretended that it means *slave*. These cases shall be examined. But before reaching that point, the facts amount to al-

most a moral demonstration, that the inspired penmen did not mean to spread a justification of human bondage upon the record.
There was a word which appropriately expressed a chattel slave which they have never used, but have always used a word which
properly express the condition of free persons in the voluntary service of another,
whether as a common laborer, a personal at-
tendant, an agent, or a public officer, represent ng some higher authority, human or divine.

Is it not clear then that they did not design to teach the rightful existence of human
chattelship.

As the writers of the New Testament have
not used the word *andrapodon* which most
specifically signifies a slave, so have they not
used the properly corresponding word, *an-
drapodismos*, which in the specific word for
slavery. As they use the word *doulos*, for
the man, the servant, which may. denote a
voluntary servant, one employed for pay ; so
they use the derivative word *douloo* to denote
the condition, the service, servitude or bondage, which may also be voluntary.

So, when speaking of rightful relations,
they have never used the word *andrapodistees*,
which signifies a slaveholder, one who reduces men to slavery, or holds them as slaves,
and which corresponds to *andrapodon*, a slave ;
but have used the word *despotees*, which signifies lord, master, or head of a family, without at all implying a chattel slaveholder.
The proper word for a slaveholder *andrapodistees*, occurs but once in the New Testament.

1 Tim. i. 10 : where it is translated *manstealers*.

Despotees, the only word used which it can be pretended means slaveholder, occurs in only ten texts in the New Testament, in six of which it is applied to God, or to Jesus Christ, and in four to men as masters. The cases in which it is applied to God or to Jesus Christ, are as follows :

"Lord, [*Despotees*,] now lettest thou thy servant, [*doulos*] depart in peace." Luke ii. 29.

"Lord, [*Despotees*] thou art God." Acts iv. 24.

"If a man therefore purge himself from these, he shall be a vessel unto honor, sanctified, and meet for his master's [*despotees*] use." 2 Tim. ii. 21.

"Denying the Lord [*Despotees*] that bought them." 2 Peter ii. 1.

"Denying the only Lord [*Despotees*] God." Jude 4.

"How long O Lord, [*Despotees*,] holy and true."

The above use of the word shows that it does not signify a slaveholder, and from the examination of the several words concerned, it appears as though the apostles were so guided as to employ none of the words which belong properly to the system of chattel slavery. The four remaining texts in which the word *despotees* occurs, are the texts which some suppose describe slavery, and these shall all be examined in their place. I have thus far proved that the inspired writers have not used one of the words which unequivocally express chattle slavery, and the fact that there

were such words in the language in which
they wrote, and that they always avoided
them, and used words which properly denote
free laborers, is very conclusive evidence
that they never designed to endorse the system, if they knew any thing about it, and
lived and labored among it.

CHRIST IN NO INSTANCE TAUGHT OR JUSTIFIED SLAVERY.

We are now prepared to enter upon an examination of the texts which it is affirmed
justify slavery.

"There came unto him a centurion, be-
seeching him and saying, Lord my servant
lieth at home sick of the palsy, grievously
tormented. And Jesus saith unto him, I will
come and heal him. The centurian answered
and said, Lord, I am not worthy that thou
shouldst come under my roof, but speak the
word only and my servant shall be healed.
For I am a man under authority, having soldiers under me : and I say to this man go,
and he goeth ; and to another come, and he
cometh ; and to my servant do this, and he
doeth it." Matt. viii. 6–9.

There is certainly no slavery in this text,
and I should not have considered it necessary
to have introduced it but for the purpose of
presenting a specimen of each class.

Slavery is not found in the fact that as a
Roman officer he had soldiers under him, that
he said to one go, and goeth ; and to another
come and he cometh. Those soldiers were
not his slaves. Nor is slavery found in the

fact that he had servants, for the word here translated servant never means slave. The word is *pais* and signifies " a child, mail or female, and of any age from infancy to manhood, a son or daughter, a boy, youth, girl, maiden."

A few examples whill show this. Matt. ii. 16. '· Herod sent forth and slew all the *children*." Here the same word is translated children. Matt. xvii. 18. " And the *child* was cured from that very hour." Here the same word is rendered child. Matt. xxi. 15. " The *children* crying in the market." Here the same word is translated children. Luke ii. 43. " The *child* Jesus tarried behind." It will not be pretended that the words *Insous ho pais*, " the child Jesus," denotes a slave, and yet the word here rendered *child*, is the same that is rendered *servant* where the centurian said " my *servant* lieth at home sick." It was probably the centurian's child that was sick ; at least it would have been just as faithful a translation to have so rendered it.

" Who then is a faithful and wise servant, whom his Lord hath made ruler over his household, to give them meat in due season ? Blessed is that servant whom the Lord, when he cometh, shall find so doing. Verily I say unto you, that he shall make him ruler over all his goods. But, and if that evil servant shall say in his heart, My lord delayeth his coming : and shall begin to smite his fellow servants, and to eat and drink with the drunken : the lord of that servant shall come in a day when he looketh not for him, and in an hour that he is not aware of, and shall cut him asunder, and appoint him his portion with the hypocrites : there shall be weeping and gnashing of teeth." Matt. xxiv. 45–51.

This is as strong a text in support of the idea of slavery as any thing found in the teachings of our Lord. I will then examine it as a decisive text by which the question may be settled.

1. Here the word rendered servant is *doulos*, which does not of itself prove the existence of slavery. This has already been proved. If then the text proves the existence of slavery it must be from some other circumstances.

2. If there is any slavery in the case, the ruling servant was a slave in common with the rest, for he is represented as smiting his fellow servants. This furnishes strong presumptive proof that none were slaves. It is unknown to the history of slavery for a chattel slave to be left in sole charge of such an immense estate as is involved in this illustration of our Lord. The management of a plantation or an estate of slaves is never left to one of the slaves, during the long and uncertain absence of the proprietor, as must have been the case if our Lord borrowed his illustration from slavery.

3. The smiting his fellow servants is no proof that they were slaves. It was a wrongful smiting, a wicked smiting, and cannot prove that either party were slaves. A hired overseer would be just as likely to smite hired laborers, as a slave overseer would be to smite slave laborers, there being nothing

to justify the smiting. Moreover the smiting
in this case is associated with drunkenness,
and hence, it is clearly just that kind of as-
sault and battery which a drunken overseer
would commit upon those who might be under his direction.

4. The punishment inflicted upon the unfaithful servant proves that he was not a
slave. It is clear that he was executed, or
cut off, which is in perfect harmony with the
customs that prevailed among eastern petty
tyrants. But as a general rule, men would
not treat an unfaithful slave in such a manner, but would rather sell him upon some
cotton or sugar plantation, or send him into
the chained gang.

5. If it were admitted that the lord was
a slaveholder, and that the servants were
slaves, it would be no justification of slavery.
It is only an illustration, and does not prove
the rightfulness of the facts and circumstances from which it is borrowed. If the fact
that our Lord used the conduct of masters
and slaves to illustrate his truths, proves
that slavery is right, much more must the
cited fact that the master cut his slave asunder prove that it is right for slaveholders to
cut down their slaves, when they disobey
them, or when they do wrong. The two
strong points in the parable are first, the servant was unfaithful and violated his charge ;
and secondly his Lord or master, severely
punished him for it. Allow this to have
transpired between a slave owner and a slave
and if its use by our Lord, to illustrate the
wicked conduct of sinners and the punish-

ment which God will inflict, proves that
slavery was right, it must prove with equal
certainty that the punishment inflicted by the
master was right. That was capital punishment ; he cut him asunder. The truth is, the
use our Lord makes of the facts is no endorsement of the slavery or of the particular conduct of the master, upon the supposition that there is any slavery in the case.
Christ often employed facts and translations
to illustrate the truth, without endorsing
such facts and illustrations. A few examples
will show this. The parable of the vine-
yard recorded Matt. xxi. 33–41, is of this
class. It does not endorse the act of the
proprietor in destroying the husband-men.
The parable of the marriage supper recorded, Matt. xxii. 1–14, is of the same class.
It does not prove the rightfulness even of
making such a feast, much less does it justify
the conduct of the king in dealing so severely with the man who had not on a wedding
garment. That man was merely guilty of
an impropriety, which could not justify such
severe punishment ; but our Saviour could
use the fact to illustrate a righteous administration without endorsing it. The case of
the unjust steward, recorded Luke xvi. 1–9,
is entirely conclusive on this point. It cannot be presumed that Christ intended to endorse the conduct of that steward as morally right.

Enough has been said, not only to show
that the text with which I started contains
no justification of slavery, but also to show
that no other like text found among our Sa-

viour's parables and illustrations can be tortured into a support of chattel bondage.
We may therefore leave the gospels and turn
to the epistles and see if slavery can be found
in them.

PAUL TO THE CORINTHIANS DOES NOT JUSTIFY SLAVERY.

" Let every man abide in the same calling
wherein he was called. Art thou called,
being a servant? Care not for it; but if
thou mayest be made free use *it* rather. For
he that is called in the Lord, *being* a servant,
is the Lord's freeman : likewise also he that
is called *being* free, is Christ's servant. Ye
are bought with a price, be not ye the servants of men. Brethren, let every man wherein he is called, therein abide with God."
Cor. vii. 20-22.

This text may refer to slavery, the persons
here called servants, *doulos*, may have been
slaves. It is not certain that they were
slaves because they are called *doulos*, for this
term is often applied to free persons who are
merely in the employ of another. The fact
is admitted that slavery did exist in that
country, and that the word doulos might be
applied to a slave, just as our word servant,
is used to denote any one who serves, whether voluntary or involuntary, free or bond.
This is all the concession candor requires me
to make, and in this lies all the proof there
is that slavery is involved in the case. The
text upon its face contains several things

which are unfavorable to the idea that the persons treated of were chattel slaves. I urge two grounds of defense against any conclusion drawn from the text, that slavery is or can be right.

I. It is not clear that the persons were slaves, to whom the apostle wrote. This is a vital point and must be positively proved; inference or mere probability will not do in such a case. Here is a great system of human bondage, sought to be justified, and of course, no text can be admitted as proving it right, unless it be certain that it relates to the subject. Now, where is the proof that this text certainly speaks of slaves.

1. The use of the word, *doulos*, does not prove it, for that is applied to Jesus Christ, Paul and Peter, to all christians, and to free persons who are in the employ of others, whether as public officers or mere laborers.

2. The general instruction given does not prove that the persons addressed were slaves. The general instruction is for all to abide in the same calling they were in when converted. The same principle is applied specifically to husbands and wives, as well as to servants. The general instruction therefore does not prove that slaves are meant.

3. The specific application of this instruction to servants by name, does not prove that they were slaves. It might be necessary to give such instruction to free or hired servants. The gospel was making inroads upon a heathen community, and it may be presumed that the greatest portion of the converts

were among the lower classes and servants.
If these servants were all to forsake their
positions and the employ of all unconverted
employers, so soon as they were converted,
it would not only produce confusion and
much inconvenience, but bring Christianity
into discredit and provoke persecution. It
would not only deprive many families of the
requisit number of laborers, but would throw
an equal number of laborers out of employ.

4. The exception which the apostle makesto
the specific application of his general rule to
servants,does not prove that they were slaves.
The exception is this, " But if thou mayest
be made free, use it rather." This is doubtless the strongest point in support of slavery
contained in the text, for those who must find
slavery in it somehow, will at once say that
it supposes that they might not be able to be
free, in which case they must be slaves.
This is plausible, but it is not a necessary
conclusion, and therefore cannot be allowed
as establishing the rightfulness of slavery.
It may refer to contracts and relations voluntarily entered into for a limited term of
years, and for a price stipulated. Such cases exist in every community, and where a
considerable portion of an entirely heathen
community, should suddenly embrace christianity, some of the converts would be found
sustaining these relations, and involved in
these obligations to heathen parties entirely
unfriendly to the spiritual interest of such
converts. Now, though it would not be
proper to violently rupture all such contracts
on the conversion of one of the parties.

though it would be a good general rule for every man to abide in his calling or occupation, yet where a release could be peaceably obtained in any such case, it would be best to improve it. This is all that the text necessarily means, and this is rendered the more probable sense, from the fact that, if they were really slaves, and their state of slavery regarded as right in the light of the gospel, the probability of obtaining a release would hardly be great enough to constitute the bassis of a special apostolic rule. Indeed, the exposition is more consistent with the whole scope of the apostle's reasoning than any exposition that can be based upon the assumption that chattel slavery was the thing with which the apostle was dealing.

II. Allowing that the text does treat of slaves, that the person named as "called being a servant," was a personal chattel, it does not prove slavery to be right, or throw over it any sanction, not even by implication.— The former exposition is doubtless the right one, upon the supposition that the persons were not slaves, but upon the supposition that they were slaves, that exposition is set aside, and one entirely different must be resorted to. No such exposition can be adopted as will make the text approve of slavery.

1. The direction, "let every man abide in the same calling wherein he is called," does not teach the duty of a voluntary submission to slavery, upon the supposition that the direction was given to slaves; and unless it teaches the duty of voluntary submission to slavery, it does not and cannot prove slavery

to be right.   The words, " If thou mayest be
free, use it rather," are just as positive
and binding as the words, " let every man
abide in the same calling," and allowing the
words to be addressed to slaves, they command every christian convert, who is a slave,
to obtain his freedom if he can ; it leaves him
no right to consent to be a slave, if he may
be free ; if he has power to be free.

The word here translated *mayest* is *dunamai*
and is translated in this case by too soft a term
to do justice to the original in this connection.   It is used to express a thing possible
or impossible in the most absolute sense.—
It occurs in about two hundred and ten texts
and is uniformly translated *can* and with a
negative particle *cannot*, *able* and not *able*,
and in very few cases, not over five in all, it
is rendered *may* ; once it is rendered *might*,
and in only one case besides the text, is rendered *mayest*.   That is Luke xvi. 2.   " Thou
mayest be no longer steward." Here a stronger word would do better justice to the sense.
The word occurs in such texts as the following : " God is *able* of these stones to raise up
children unto Abraham."   Matt. iii. 9.

" A city that is set on a hill *can*not be
hid." v. 14.

Thou *canst* not make one hair white or
black." 36.

" No man *can* serve two masters." vi. 24.

" But *are* not *able* to kill the soul."   x. 28.

" From which ye *could* not be justified by
the law of Moses."   Acts xiii. 39.

" They that are in the flesh *can*not please
God."   Rom. viii. 8.

" To him *that is of power* to establish you."
xvi. 25.

The word is supposed to be derived fron
deinos, powerful, and hence in the expression
" If thou *mayest* be free, the sense is, if thou
hast power to be free, if thou hast strength
to be free, if thou art able to be free, if thou
canst be free, " use it rather."

There can be no doubt of this position,
that the text leaves those concerned no choice
between slavery and liberty ; if it refers to
slaves, it requires them to take and use their
liberty if they can get it, leaving no right to
remain in the condition of slaves any longer
than up to the time they can be free. This
is very important in two points of light.

1. It is a most clearly implied condemnation of slavery as unfriendly to the develope-
ment of Christianity in the heart and life.—
This of itself proves that the text does not
and cannot justify slavery.

2. This positive command requiring the
slave to take and use his liberty, whenever
he can get it, necessarily qualifies and limits
what is said of abiding in the condition
wherein they were called. "Let every man
abide in the same calling where he was called.
Art thou called, being a servant ? Care not
for it, but if thou mayest be made free, use
it rather." The sense must be that the slave
was to abide in slavery as a Christian, until
he could be made free, rather than to give up
his Christianity on the ground that a slave
must first be made free before he could be a
Christian. The obligation was to be a
Christian while he was compelled to remain
a slave, rather than to remain a slave one

hour after he could be free.   To abide in the
same calling wherein he was called, means
that he should remain a christian in that condition, until he can get out of it rather than
waiting until he can get out of it before he
undertakes to be a christian.   The fact that
the slave is commanded to use his freedom
if he can be made free, forbids any other construction than that which I have put upon
the words.   The command to use his liberty
if he can be made free, limits the command
to abide as he was called, to the sense of
submitting to slavery as an unavoidable evil,
until he can get out of it in a manner consistent with the laws of Christianity.   This
is all the obligation that is imposed upon
the slave, and this is not the slightest justification of slavery, for there is not a christian
anti-slavery man in the country, even the
most ultra, who would not now give the same
advice to all slaves in the land, could they
speak in their ears.   Advice or a command
to submit to a wrong which we have not power to prevent, is no justification of that wrong.
"But I say unto you that ye resist not evil,"
is no justification of evil.   The fact that
"charity beareth all things," and "endureth
all things," does not prove that all things
thus borne and endured are right.   So no
command, were it ever so plain, to submit, ever so quietly to slavery, as a condition from
which we have no power to escape, could be
a justification of slavery.

It strikes me that we are compelled to this
explanation of the text, to save the apostle
from confusion and self contradiction, if we
admit that he was really treating of chattel

slavery. We cannot suppose that the apostle uses the same word in two or more different senses in the same most intimate connection, without giving any intimation of the fact; if therefore we render the word *doulos*, slave, instead of servant, we must preserve this rendering through the whole connection. In that case the text will read thus: "Let every man abide in the same calling where he was called. Art thou called being **a** *slave* care not for it: but if thou mayest be made free use it rather. For he that is called in the Lord being a *slave* is the Lord's *freeman*: likewise, he also that is called being *free* is Christ's *slave*. Ye are bought with a price; be not ye the *slaves* of men."

This makes the apostle assert that a converted slave is a slave of man, and God's free man at the same time. This is impossible, for if the obligations of slavery are morally binding on the slave, he cannot be free to serve God; but if the slavery be an entire unmingled moral wrong, imposing no moral obligation on the slave, but only a physical restraint, then can the slave be God's free man, just as clearly as he whose feet and hands should be paralized, could still be God's free man, his head and heart being still sound.

Again, the assumption that the apostle is treating of chattel slavery, as the text is above rendered, makes him assert that the converted *slave* is God's free man, and that the converted free man is God's *slave*. If by servitude a voluntary state is meant, in which case there is no chattel slavery: or if chattel slavery be understood, as a human crime.

inflicted upon them by force, imposing no moral obligation, then the whole is consistent.

Finally, the idea that chattel slavery is involved, and that slaves are under moral obligation to submit to it, as per corresponding moral right on the part of the slaveholder to hold them as slaves, makes the apostle command them to abide in slavery and not to abide in it ; to be slaves and not to be at the same time. The sense must run thus,—"Let every man abide in the same calling wherein he is called," that is, if a man is called being a slave, let him remain a slave; but as " ye are bought with a price, be not ye the *slaves* of men." A more direct and palpable contradiction could not be perpetrated. But allow that there is no justification of slavery, that slaves are only directed to submit to it and bear it as a physical necessity which they have no power to escape, and the whole is plain and consistent, then may they be required to abide in it and endure all its wrongs as Christians, until providence shall open a way for them to escape from it.

I have bestowed full attention to the above text, because it is believed to be one of the strongest in support of slavery, and because it is the first of the class with which I have undertaken to grapple. In disposing of it, I have settled some principles, which can be applied in the consideration of other texts, without having to be again discussed at length.

PAUL TO THE EPHESIANS HAS NOT SANCTIONED SLAVERY.

"Servants, be obedient to them that are your masters, according to the flesh, with fear and trembling, in singleness of your heart, as unto Christ; not with eye-service, as men-pleasers; but as the servants of Christ, doing the will of God from the heart; with good will doing service, as to the Lord, and not to men; knowing that whatsoever good thing any man doeth, the same shall he receive of the Lord, whether he be bond or free. And, ye masters, do the same things unto them, forbearing threatening: knowing that your Master also is in heaven; neither is there respect of persons with him". Eph. vi. 5–9.

This is another of the strongest texts urged by the advocates of slavery, in support of the terrible institution. On the examination of each of these texts, two principle questions, are necessarily raised, viz: first, does the text treat of slaves, slaveholders and slavery? and secondly, if so, does it sanction slavery as morally right? Unless both these questions are clearly and undeniably answered in the affirmative, the argument for slavery must fall. We say then of this text:

I. It is not certain that the persons here called servants, were chattel slaves; and that the persons called masters, were slaveholders.

1. It does not follow that slaves and slaveholders are treated of from the terms employ-

ed. The word here translated servants is
douloi, the plural of *doulos*. That this word
of itself does not prove that chattel slaves are
meant, has been already sufficiently shown.

The word masters is *kurioi*, the plural of
kurios. It has been sufficiently shown that
this word does not necessarily mean a slaveholder. I will however add two examples of
its use.

"The same Lord, (*Kurios*,) over all is rich
unto all that call upon him." Rom. x. 12.
Here the word is used to denote the Supreme
Ruler of all men.

"Sirs, (*Kurioi*, plural of *Kurios*,) what must
I do to be saved." Here the word is used as
a mere title or sign of respect, and can mean
no more than our English words, Sirs, Gen-
tlemen, or Mister. The use of the word
therefore, cannot prove that slaveholders are
intended.

2. The duties enjoined upon these servants,
does not prove that they were slaves. Not a
word is said which will not apply as appropriately to free hired laborers as to slaves.

(1.) The command to obey them that were
their masters, does not prove the existence
of chattel slavery. This must follow from
two considerations. First, their obedience
was limited to what was morally right. This
is clear from the fact that their obedience
was to be rendered "as the servants of Christ,
doing the will of God from the heart." This
limits obedience to the will of God, and
makes the actor the judge of what that will
is, which is inconsistent with chattel slavery.
Secondly, with this limitation, obedience is

due to all employers, and all free persons who
engage in the service of others, are bound to
obey them, and carry out all their orders, according to the usages of the community, within the limits of the will of God, or what is
morally right.   Such a direction, to a community, newly converted from heathenism,
and still intermingled with the unconverted
heathen, must have been necessary, and its
observance essential to the reputation and future success of the gospel among them.   It is
clear then that the simple command that servants obey does not prove that they were
slaves.

(2.) The qualifying words added to the
word masters, "according to the flesh," do not
prove the existence of the relation of owner
and slave. TheGreek word,*sarks*, here rendered *flesh*, literally signifies the human body in
contradistinction from the spirit or mind.

Matthew Henry construes it thus : "Who
have the command of your bodies, but not of
your souls : God above has dominion over
these."

Dr. A. Clark thus : "Your masters in secular things ; for they have no authority over
your religion nor over your souls."

Rev. A. Barnes, thus : "This is designed,
evidently to limit the obligation. The meaning is, that they had control over the body,
the flesh. They had the power to command
the service which the body could render ; but
they were not lords of the spirit. The soul
acknowledges God as its Lord, and to the
Lord they were to submit in a higher sense
than to their masters." Allow either of these

expositions, and there can be no slavery made out of the text. If there be a limit to the slave's obedience, and if the slave is judge of that limit, as he must be, for the language is addressed to him, to govern his conduct, then there is an end to slavery. But if we understand free men under contract to serve others, it is all plain. The limitation, "according to the flesh," must mean, obey them in secular matters only, and so far only as does not conflict with the spiritual or moral claims of Christianity. It left them no right to serve or to agree to serve beyond what was consistent with their obligations and duties as Christians.

(3.) The manner of rendering the obedience required does not prove the existence of chattel slavery. The manner was "with fear and trembling."

The words, *phobou kai tromou*, fear and trembling, are capable of a great latitude of meaning, from absolute terror to a religious veneration, or the respect due to any superior. The same expression occurs in two other texts. The first is 2 Cor. vii. 15, where Paul says of Titus, "with fear and trembling, *phobou kai tromou*, ye received him."

The other text is Phil. ii. 12. "Work out your own salvation with fear and trembling, *phobou kai tromou*." In this text fear and trembling means deep solicitude or apprehension.

The Greek word *phobou*, which is the genitive singular of *phobos*, is defined thus : "Fear, dread, terror, fright, apprehension, alarm, flight, rought." If it be understood in its mildest sense, as *fear* in the sense of anxiety, reverence or respect, or *apprehension*, in the sense of uneasiness of mind, lest by failing to obey, they should injure the reputation of the gospel, it is all perfectly consistent with the position and duties of free hired servants. And this is all that the word necessarily means. The same word is used to express the respect which wives are required to manifest towards their husbands. "Wives be in subjection to your own husbands; that if any obey not the word, they also may without the word be won by the conversation of the wives; while they behold your chaste conversation coupled with *fear*.". 1 Peter iii. 1, 2. Here the same word is used in the original translated *fear*. If the words, *phobou kai tromou* be understood in any higher sense, which renders it inapplicable to free hired laborers, as dread, terror, or fright, it renders the whole matter inconsistent with a Christian brotherhood, and makes the scriptures contradict themselves. No Christian can be justified in holding his brother Christian under his own reign of terror, which makes him afraid, and causes him to tremble at the sound of his footsteps, or the tone of his voice, or the flash of his eye. "Fear and trembling," in such a sense, is inconsistent with what is said to the masters. This will be clearly seen hereafter. It is only necessary at this point to remark that slaves would not be likely to fear and tremble before masters, who were not allowed even to threaten them. It would make the scriptures contradict themselves, for it is written, "There is no fear in love; but perfect love casteth out

fear ; because fear hath torment." 1 John.
iv. 18. Such are the difficulties, if we understand the language, "fear and tremble," in
the sense in which slaves fear and tremble in
the South ; but if we understand it in the
milder sense in which I have explained it
above, and in which sense it isapplicable to
free laborers, and to wives as shown, the
whole matter will appear plain. It must appear from what has been said that there is
nothing in the duties enjoined which proves
the existence of slavery.

3. The discrimination between bond and
free, does not prove the existence of slavery.
As an encouragement to faithful servants,
Paul says, "whatsoever good thing any man
doeth, the same shall he receive of the Lord,
whether he be *bond* or *free.* This does not
add the slightest force to the argument, for
the word that is rendered *bond*, is the same
that is rendered servant in the 5th verse. It
is *doulos ; doulos eite eleutheros ;* bond or free.
"Whether he be servant or free, would be a
translation more in accordance with common
usuage. The word *doulos,* servant, occurs
over one hundred and twenty times in theNew
Testament, and in every instance is translated servant, save seven in which it is rendered bond. Four of the seven exceptions occur
in the writings of Paul, and the text under
consideration is the only one which can be
supposed to justify slavery in any sense. The
other three are as follows: "For by one
Spirit are we all baptized into one body,
whether Jews or Gentiles, whether *bond or
free.*" 1 Cor. xii. 13. "There is neither

Jew nor Greek, neither *bond nor free."* Gal. iii. 28. "And have put on the new man, which is renewed in knowledge after the image of him that created him : where there is neither Greek nor Jew, circumcision nor uncircumcision, Barbarian, Scythian, *bond nor free."* Col. iii. 10, 11. If the word *doulos,* rendered bond in these texts, means a chattel slave, the thing cannot exist among Christians, and the gospel abolishes the relation of master and slave so soon as the parties are converted. The other three cases in which the word *doulos* is translated bond, are in revelations. They need not be examined, as they have no important bearing on the question. We see from the above the discrimination between bond and free does not prove the existence of chattel slavery, because it is perfectly appropriate to distinguish between men who are the servants of others, as hired laborers, and who are not. It only has the force of the word servant in contradistinction from one who is an employer, or who labors for himself.

4. The obligations imposed upon the masters does not prove that they were chattel slaveholders, or that their servants were their chattel slaves. I know not how to reconcile what is said to the masters with the possibility that chattel slavery is involved. This however is not my part of the enterprise, my work is to show that what is said does not prove that slavery existed, and if in doing this, I prove that it did not exist, it will be the result of the nature of the facts I have to deal with. Two things are commanded for which a reason is assigned.

(1.) Masters are commanded to " do the same things unto them," that is to their servants. What is here meant by "the same things." It certainly refers to what had been said to servants. It will not admit of a strict literal construction, for that would require the master to obey the servant with fear and trembling ; it would be to put the servant and the master upon an exact equality in all things. This we know the apostle did not mean, and to attempt to ground an argument upon such a literal sense, would be to appear uncandid. "The same things," in the connection, literally means just what he had been telling the servants to do, but from this we must depart, but we are not allowed to depart from the literal sense only so far as to reach. a sense which will be in harmony with the general scope of the subject. Let us try it. Suppose we understand by the same things, that Paul merely meant to command masters to act towards their servants, upon the same principles upon which he had commanded the servants to act towards them ; or in other words, that Paul meant to command masters to pursue a course of conduct towards their servants, which correspond to the conduct which he had commanded the servants to pursue towards them.

This strikes me as not only a fair and liberal view, but as the only true view. A slaveholder cannot deny the fairness of this construction of the words. Now let me apply the principle. It will run thus :

"Servants be obedient to them that are your masters." Masters give no oppressive, unreasonable, or morally wrong commands. Then must the servant be left free to serve his God, and discharge all the domestic duties of a husband, father, wife, mother, son or daughter. This would make an end of chattel slavery.

Servants obey with fear and tremble, that is with all due respect for superiors. Masters, treat your servants with all the gentleness and kindness that is due from a superior to an inferior. This even cannot be reconciled with chattel slavery. Servants, serve in singleness of heart, as unto Christ. Masters, conduct yourselves towards your servants with entire honesty, and pay them for their labor as doing it unto Christ.

Servants, serve " not with eye-service as man pleasers, but as the servants of Christ." Masters, do not treat your servants in the presence of others with apparent kindness to secure a good name, and then abuse them when there is no one to see or hear ; but treat them with the same honesty and purity of motive with which you serve Christ.

Servants, obey as doing the will of God from the heart. Masters command and claim nothing which is contrary to the will of God.

There is certainly no slavery in all this, but much which appears inconsistent with slavery. It would not be sufficient to say that it might refer to slavery, or that it might be reconciled with slavery ; it must positively mean slavery beyond a doubt to be admitted as proof of the rightful existence of slavery in this land and age, for that is the real question.

(2.) Masters are commanded to forbear threatning. This does not prove that Paul was treating of chattel slaveholders and slaves. This forbids all punishment, all chastizement. No construction can be put upon the words which will make them less restrictive.

The Greek word *anieemi*, here rendered *forbearing*, has a variety of significations and shades of meaning, among which are the following. " To remit, forgive, forbear ; to dismiss, leave, let alone ; to desert, forsake ; to let slip, omit, neglect." The word occurs but four times in the New Testament as follows : Acts xvi. 26, where it is translated *loosed*. " Every ones hands were *loosed*."— Acts xxvii. 40. it is again translated *loosed*. " They committed themselves unto the sea, and *loosed* the rudder-bands, and hoisted up the mainsail to the wind." Heb. xiii. 5, it is translated *will leave*, being accompanied with a negative, *never*. " He hath said, I *will* never *leave* thee nor forsake thee."

The only remaining case is the text under consideration, where it is translated *forbearing*, threatening. There is seen to be nothing in the use of the word in other texts, to make it mean less here than a command not to threaten at all. He who threatens in any degree does not forbear threatening.

The word, *threatening*, denotes the act of making a declaration of an intention to inflict punishment. It is used in no other sense. It occurs but four times in the New Testament. Acts iv. 17. " But that it spread no further among the people, let us strictly threaten them." The Greek words are, *apiles apilesometha*, a literal translation of which would be, " Let us threaten them with threatening." In the twenty-ninth verse, it is said, " And now Lord behold their *threatenings.*" The other text where the word occurs is Acts ix. 1. " And Saul yet breathing out threatenings," *apilees*, threatenings. It is clear then that the word *forbearing*, as used in the text, means not to do, or refrain from doing ; and the word, threatening, means the making a declaration of a purpose to inflict punishment. The two words, therefore as connected in the text, amount to a command not to threaten punishment. This by the most certain implication forbids the punishment itself. It would be absurd to suppose christian slaveholders were allowed to inflict a punishment, which they were forbidden to threaten. It is certain then in the case of the masters and servants here treated of, the masters were not allowed by the law of Christianity to inflict any punishment upon their servants, for they were not allowed even to threaten them.   This principle carried out, would make an end of chattel slavery, such is human nature, under every modification yet known, that chattel slavery can be maintained only by physical force, which holds the slave in constant dread of punishment, and which amounts to a constant warfare, not only upon his skin, but upon his life.

5. The reason assigned for the commands given to the masters is very far from proving that they were slaveholders, or that their servants were chattel slaves.   This reason is

thus stated, " Knowing that your Master is
also in heaven ; neither is there respect of
persons with him." The word, Master, here
is the same as in the direction, only here it is
singular, *kurios*, and there it is plural, *kurioi*.
Translate it slaveholder and it would read
thus : " Ye *slaveholders*, do the same things unto them ; knowing that your *slaveholder* also
is in heaven." Or more correctly, " ye *owners*, do the same things unto them ; knowing
that your *owner* also is in heaven." Every
one must know that this does not express the
true sense of the apostle. The meaning is,
that they were to conduct themselves justly
and kindly towards their servants, or inferi-
ors, because they were the servants of God,
to whom they must render an account for
their conduct. Now the word *kurios* not only means God as a name of the Supreme Being, but it also signifies a ruler. It is derived from *kuros*, authority. Translate it by
ruler and the whole connection will be consistent. " And ye *rulers* do the same things
unto them ; knowing that your *ruler* is in
heaven." It would be a good translation to
render it lord, thus, " And ye *lords*, do the
same things unto them ; knowing that your
Lord also is in heaven." It is so translated in
several texts. It is thus rendered in the
parable of the talents, Matt. xxiv. 14–30.
" After a long time the *lord* of those servants
cometh." Many other cases might be cited
where it is thus rendered. In the reason
then, so far as regards the fact that they have
a master in heaven, slavery gets no support.

But what is affirmed of the master in heav-

en, as an additional reason for the command,
does not favor slavery. "Neither is there
respect of persons with him." These masters
were admonished to conduct themselves properly towards their servants, because there
was no respect of persons with their master
in heaven.   It appears to me this reason destroys the idea of slavery, and proves that
no such unequal relation can rightfully exist
among Christians.   The expression, respect
of persons, comes from the Greek word, *pro-
sopoleepsia*, the clear and undeniable sense of
which is, that God, their master in heaven,
regarded the two clases of persons here
named, masters and servants, just alike, giving them equal rights, and governing them
on equal principles.   It means that God does
not favor one more than another.   It means
nothing less and nothing more, and nothing
else.   The word is thus briefly defined, "an
excepting of or respect of persons, partiality."
It appears to me that God cannot sanction
chattel slavery, without being a respecter of
persons, or being partial.   The charge does
not lie against other destinctions and differ-
ences which exist among men.   One is poor,
and another is rich, but they all have the
same right to seek and gain riches, and the
riches on one hand and the poverty on the
other, are often the result of human actions
which God condemns.   But if slavery be
right, men are made slaves prospectively before they are born, by a rule of God's moral
government, and without any reference to
their prospective conduct, and they are born
into the world without the right to seek for

themselves the common advantages of life.
If God be the author of this ; if he has con-
ferred upon one class of persons, the right to
lay their hands upon another class as they
come into the world, and appropriate them to
their own use and behoof, there is respect of
persons with God, the very thing which Paul
denies in addressing masters, as the ground
of the commands he gives them. Thus is it
seen that the reason which the apostle assigns
for his directions cuts up the foundation principle of chattel slavery, and destroys the
system root and branch.

I have now shown that the text under consideration does not contain slavery, that it is
not clear that it treats of the thing at all, and
I will pass to notice briefly the second point.

II.   If it were admitted that the text treats
of slavery, it does not follow that slavery is
right, for it in no sense justifies the necessary
assumptions of a chattel slaveholder.

1. The directions given to the servants is
no more than might be given to chattel slaves
as a means of promoting their own interests,
without the slightest endorsement of the masters right to hold them. Suppose a man to
be held wrongfully as a slave, without the
power to escape from the grasp of his oppressor, what would a friend advise him to do ?
Just what the apostle has commanded in the
case before us.   I would say, obey your master in every thing that the law of Christianity will allow you to do, and obey with visible
fear and trembling, for such a course is the
only means of securing such treatment as
will render life endurable.   Self interest

would not only dictate such a course, but duty to God would demand it. Christians are bound to pursue a course, within the limits of what may and may not be done, as will render their own lives most peaceful and comfortable, and enable them to be most useful to their fellow creatures in leading them to embrace the same blessed Christianity. With a slave, unable to escape from his chains, such a course would be just the one pointed out by the apostle in the text under consideration. And it is a very striking fact that the apostle makes no appeal to the master's rights as a reason for his directions, but appeals exclusively to the duty they owe to God. He even goes so far as to exclude all together the master with all of his supposed rights from the considerations and motives that are to govern them in their obedience. They are not to do it "as men-pleasers, but as the servants of Christ doing the will of God from the heart ; with good will doing service, as to the Lord and not to men." If they were not to do the service as to men, it must follow that men had no rightful claim on those service, and the obedience is commanded not because slavery is right, but because under the circumstances, it was necessary to promote their own comfort and the interests of Christianity. Upon the supposition that there was real chattel slavery involved, there is not the slightest endorsement of the system found in the directions given to the servants. And surely it should be found in the directions given to the servants, if any where. If slavery be a heaven ordained institution, it might appear neces-

sary to teach the slaves that it is right,
and that they owe service to their masters,
but it would hardly be necessary to teach
masters that they had a right to hold their
slaves, least they should let them go. I say
therefore that if there is any justification of
slavery, it should be found in the directions
given to the servants, and yet there is not the
slightest intimation that they owe their masters' service, but they are forbidden to do service as to men, but are required to do it as
to God. The fact then that there is not the
slightest justification of slavery in the directions given to the servants, renders it quite
clear that the apostle did not design to justify slavery.

2. There is no justification of slavery found
in the directions given to the masters, upon
the supposition that they were chattel slaveholders. What they are commanded to do
was undoubtedly right, but there is not a
word said in these commands which implies
that it is right to hold a fellow being as a
chattel slave. The argument for slavery does
not depend so much upon what is said to the
masters as upon what is not said, and upon
assumed facts. The argument is this; they
were slaveholders, and members of the church,
and the apostle wrote to them, giving rules
for the regulation of their conduct as masters, and did not command them to emancipate their slaves, or forbid them to hold
slaves. This, it is insisted, is an implied endorsement of slavery. This is the strongest
form that can be given to the argument, and
in this shape I will meet it in this place.

(1.) The argument is unsound because it

takes for granted the main point to be proved, viz : that they were really chattel slaveholders. The words do not prove that to be a fact. It is first taken for granted that slavery existed, and then the words are construed in the light of this assumption. As the words do not prove the existence of chattel slavery, it should be proved that it did exist, before it can be affirmed that the apostle did treat of slavery, or that slaveholders were members of the church. This, on my part, is a falling back upon a previous argument, which I do to make the argument entire in this place, and not to make it the main issue, as the reader will soon see. I have shown that there is no proof found in the text that it treats of chattel slavery. This renders the assertion that slaveholders were in the church, and hence that the apostle wrote to slaveholders, and gave them directions how to conduct themselves as such, were assumptions, a begging of the question. But I will wave this, and meet the issue upon the assumption that it was chattel slavery of which Paul treated.

(2) If it be admitted that slaveholders were members of the church at the time this epistle was written, it will not follow that it is right. Many wrong practices found their way into the church, and many persons were acknowledged members of the church who did not conform in all matters to the doctrines and precepts of Christianity. It is to be borne in mind that the best of the members were fresh converts from heathenism ; with all its dark- ness and corruptions ; that there was not per- vading the community outside of the church,

that general religious light that now pervades
the community outside of the church in this
country, and that there were not there as
many sources of light as there is now among
us, and not the same general prevalence of
education, and Christian libraries containing
the well defined fundamental principles of
morality and human duty.   Under such circumstances, the church drawing her recruits
from amid the dark corruptions of heathenism,
by sudden conversions, she could not but be
liable to a constant influx of darkness to be
enlightened, and corruption to be purged out.
If it could be proved that slaveholders were
in the church, under such circumstances, it
would not follow that it is right without a specific endorsement of the thing itself, since
many persons got into the church who were
very wrong in some of their practices.   In
writing to the Corinthian church, "unto the
church of God which is at Corinth, to them
that are sanctified in Christ Jesus ;" Paul
said, "Awake to righteousness and sin not ;
for some have not the knowledge of God : I
speak this to *your shame.*"   1 Cor. xv. 34.
Other texts might be cited to show that there
were bad men connected with the church,
and men who were partially enlightened, and
but partially reformed of their heathen practices. The fact then that a slaveholder should
be found in connection with such a church,
would not prove slaveholding to be right
without a specific endorsement.   This compels the advocate of slavery to fall back upon
the actual words of the apostle for proof that
slavery is right, leaving no ground to infer

that it is right, because he finds it in the church. But I have already proved that the words of the apostle contain no endorsement of slavery ; that in addressing servants concerning their duty, he sets up no claim of rights on behalf of the master, and that he only urges the rights of God ; and that in addressing masters, he makes no allusion to their rights as masters, but urges, on the ground of their accountibility to God, a course of conduct entirely inconsistent with chattel slavery. If these slaveholders got into church, so did other wrong doers get into the church, while Paul, in addressing these slaveholders as a specific class, commanded them to pursue a course which amounted to an entire abolition of chattel slavery. Where then is the proof that slavery is right, upon the supposition that slaveholders were in the church ? It is not found in the fact that they were in the church, because persons were in the church who practiced what is wrong ; and it is not found in the nature of the directions the apostles gave these slaveholders, for he directed them to pursue a course which was an abandonment of all coersive slavery. If then slavery is not proved to be right by the fact that it was in the church, nor yet by the apostles' directions on the subject, there is no proof in the text that it is right, allowing slavery to be the subject treated. I have now disposed of another of the strong texts claimed by the advocates of slavery, by proving first, that it is not clear that it treats of slavery, and secondly, that if it does treat of slave-

7

ry, it contains no endorsement of the practice of slaveholding.

PAUL TO THE COLLOSSIANS DOES NOT JUSTIFY SLAVERY.

"Servants, obey in all things your masters accordirg to the flesh; not with eye service as men pleasers; but in singleness of heart fearing God; and whatsoever ye do, do it heartily, as to the Lord, and not unto men; knowing that of the Lord ye shall receive the reward of the inheritance; for ye serve the Lord Christ. But he that doeth wrong, shall receive for the wrong which he hath done : and there is no respect of persons." Col. iii. 22–25.

"Masters, **give** unto your servants that which is just and equal; knowing that ye also have a master in heaven." Col. iv. 1.

These texts, though quoted from different chapters, constitute but one subject. The first verse of the fourth chapter belongs to the third chapter, and should not have been separated from it. We have then before us the direction of Paul, both to servants and masters in the same connection, and will examine the subject and see if it contains an endorsement of slavery.

The same questions are involved that have been discussed in relation to other texts, viz : does the text treat of slavery at all ? and if so, does it prove it to be right ?

This text is so nearly like Eph. vi. 5–9, in its language, which has already been examined, that on several points it will only be necessary to refer the reader to what was said upon that text. There can be no doubt from the similarity of the two passages, both being written by the same hand, that they both relate to the same class of persons. If slaveholders and slaves were treated of in the former text, they are in this. On the other hand, if I succeeded in proving that the former text does not treat of slaveholders and slaves, and that it does not justify slavery, upon the supposition that chattel slavery is involved, the same conclusion must follow in regard to the text now under consideration. It would therefore now be safe for the argument to leave this text to be understood in the light of the argument advanced upon the former. But as there are a few expressions found in this, not contained in that, I will examine it, after first naming those points which were fully explained while examining the former passage.

1. The terms, servants and masters have been sufficiently explained. It has been shown that no reliable conclusion can be drawn from the use of these terms in support of chattel slavery.

2. The qualifying adjunct, "according to the flesh," was there fully explained. The reader has only to apply the remarks there made on this expression to this text, and he will realize its force.

3. The expression, "not with eye service as men pleasers," was there explained.

4. The duty here enjoined, of obeying "in singleness of heart," and of doing their duty "as to the Lord and not unto men," was there

sufficiently discussed, and the argument need
not be repeated here

5. The declaration here found, that both,
the wrong and the right, shall be rewarded
at the hand of God, and that with him "their
is no respect of persons," was sufficiently explained in the former text, and shown to be ir-
reconcilable with chattel slavery.   On all
these points the reader can refer to the exposition already given of the preceeding text,
better than to have the matter repeated here.
This leaves but a few points, where the language varies, to be examined, to which I will
now attend.

I. It is not clear that the text was addressed to slaves and slaveholders.

1. It is not proved by the direction given
to the servants. "Servants obey in all things
your masters according to the flesh." This
is the only point of difference between this
and the former text, and it adds no force to
the argument in support of slavery.   To
obey "in all things" can mean no more than
to do every thing which is commanded, which
does not conflict with the law of God, which
is not a violation of the rules of the gospel.
To understand the words without this limitation, would hold servants under a divine obligation to commit murder at the command of
the master, to be the tormenter of father or
mother, or to submit to a base violation of
person and purity. Such cannot be the case,
and hence the command to obey in all things,
must be limited by what is right; and those
to whom belongs the work of obedience, and
not those who claim obedience, must belong

the privilege of judging what is right, or how
far the commands of masters can be obeyed
without sin against God. This limitation of
the servants obligation to obey must destroy
chattel slavery. The smallest reserve of the
right of judgment, on the part of slaves, must
destroy the foundation work of slavery. This
was shown in the examination of the preceeding text, and need not be further pressed in
this place. It is clearly seen that no command to servants, to obey their masters, can
prove the existence of chattel slavery, which
is not absolute, and without any reserve on
the part of the servant, of the right of judging
for himself what he may do, and what he may
not do. If the servant may say, I will not
sin when my master commands me to, or I
will pray to God when my master commands
me not to, there is an end of chattel slavery.
That such a limitation is implied in this text
is clear. Without this limitation, without
this reserved right on the part of the servant,
their could be no such thing as right and
wrong with the servant between him and
God ; the will of the master would be his only
law, and he could have no right to act with
reference to God. But Paul here commands
these very servants to act with reference to
God,to act, "as to the Lord and not unto men,"
and assures them that "of the Lord" they
should "receive the reward," if they do right,
and that "he that doeth wrong shall receive
for the wrong which he hath done." This
proves that God did claim the right to govern,
reward and punish these servants, and hence
that they were to obey their masters only so

far as was consistent with their higher duty to God, and the conclusion is irresistible that the directions of the apostle not only fail to prove that they were chattel slaves, but actually strike a blow at the very foundations of the system. The directions contain a principle which, like a consuming fire, must burn up and consume chattel slavery where ever the principle is applied. This principle is direct accountability to God, which the apostle here asserts, concerning these servants. Direct accountability to God, supposes a right to know the will of God, a right to judge of what that will requires, and a right to do that will. All this is implied in the words of the apostle when he commands them to act " as to God and not unto men," and assures them that they will receive of the Lord for the good or evil they do. It is clear therefore that the apostle's directions to these servants do not prove the existence of slavery, but overturn its very foundation principle.

2. The existence of slavery is not proved by what the apostle commands masters to do, "Masters, give unto your servants that which is just and equal." This does not prove that the apostle was addressing slaveholders. Here are persons called masters, and the first question in issue is, were they chattel slaveholders ? but a command to give to their servants "that which is just and equal," cannot prove it, for the same thing is required of all men towards all other men, with whom they have any deal or intercourse. It is only an application of a universal principle to a specific class, and it is just as applicable to hired

laborers and apprentices, as it is to bond slaves. The very thing required does not and cannot exist in a state of chattel slavery. Justice and equality are required, and they cannot exist in harmony with slavery, as will fully appear under my next argument. How perfectly clear is it then that Paul could not have been addressing slaves and slaveholders, and giving directions for the regulation of their conduct as such, when he ordered that which is absolutely inconsistent with the relation of slave owner and slave owned.

Having now shown sufficiently clear that there is no sufficient proof that the text under consideration has any reference to chattel slavery, I will proceed to the second general branch of my argument.

II. If it were admitted that the text was addressed specifically to slaves and slaveholders, it would not follow that slavery is right, inasmuch as it contains no justification of slavery.

Waving all that has been said, let me now examine the text upon the supposition, it was addressed to men owners and men owned, and see if there is any thing in it which can be tortured into a justification of the system.

1. The justification is not found in the command to obey. This has been fully explained and demonstrated in preceeding arguments. It might just as well be argued that when Christ says, "If any man will sue thee at the law, and takes away thy coat, let him have thy cloak also," he justifies the suing, and the taking of both, the coat and the cloak,

as to argue that slavery is right, because
slaves are required to obey.

It has been shown that the obligation to
obey is limited to what is right in itself, and
obedience, so far as it can be rendered without a violation of the law of God, is the best
course a slave can pursue, until such time as
an opportunity presents for him to obtain his
liberty.

2. The justification is not found in what
the masters are commanded to do.   Here I
meet the point, effectually.   If real slavery
did exist there, the apostle commanded its abolition.   This he did in these words; "Masters give unto your servants that which is
just and equal."   They were then first, to give
their servants that which is just.   The Greek
word, *dikaion*, the neuter of *dikaios*, is truly
rendered by our English word *just;* it signifies just, upright, righteous.   If then slavery
existed the apostle interdicted it, unless it be
first proved to be just, upright or righteous.
To assume that the apostle did not condemn
slavery, much more to assume that he justified it, when he commanded slaveholders to
give their slaves that which is just, is to beg
the whole question in debate.   The command to give them that which is just, does
not define what is just and what is not, hence,
it cannot prove that slavery is right, until it
first be proved that slavery is just.   But if
liberty be the just right of every individual,
then Paul commanded the master to give
them their liberty.   If slavery existed, it
must follow that the apostle commanded its
abolition, unless it can first be proved that

slavery is just.   This can never be done ; it
cannot be just that one man should own another man, or that one man should be compelled to serve another man all life long, without his consent and without pay.   To deny
that the apostle commands the liberation of
the slaves, if slaves they were, is to beg the
whole question in dispute, by taking it for
granted that slavery is just, the main point
which should be proved.   Allow that they
were slaveholders and slaves, and that the
apostle commands the slaveholders to give to
their slaves that which is just without intima-
ting what that is, for he lays down no rule to
determine what justice requires in the case,
and the fairest assumption in the world is that
all forced service is unjust, and that justice
requires all masters to desist from compel-
ling service against the will of the servant.
But secondly, the apostle commanded them to
give their servants that which is *equal*.   The
Greek word *isoteeta*, which is the accusative
case of *isotees* signifies equality.   It is derived
from *isos*, which signifies equal, on a level,
equal to or an equivalent : hence *isotees* which
is derived from it, signifies equality, parity,
equity, impartiality.   The word here used
occurs in but one other text in the New Testament.   It is 2 Cor. viii. 14, in which it occurs twice in the same verse, and is translated
equality in both cases.   If the reader refers to
the Greek Testament, he will find the first oc-
currence of the word in the 13th verse, as
the first half of the 14th verse in the English
version, is attached to the 13th in the Greek.
The apostle then commands slaveholders to

give to their slaves equality, or parity.   This certainly must destroy the chattel principle, and secure to the laborer a just compensation for his labor.   There is no equality, parity, equity, or impartiality, in one man's owning another, and receiving his labor without compensation.   The apostle therefore commands what cannot be reconciled with chattel slavery, and of course he did not justify it.

But waving all criticism, the simple words of the English text, "that which is just and equal," can mean no less than that which is right, that which is fairly their due, and this of itself would destroy slavery at once and forever.

I will here quote from Rev. A. Barnes' notes on the text, as his remarks fully cover this point. He says: " They were to render them that which is just and equal.   Wha would follow from this if fairly applied? What would be just and equal to a man in those circumstances ?   Would it be to compensate him fairly for his labor ; to furnish him an adequate renumeration for what he earned ?   But this would strike a blow at the root of slavery, for one of the elementary principles is, that there must be unrequited labor.

"If a man should in fact, render to his slaves that which is just and equal, would he not restore them to freedom ?   Have they not been deprived of their liberty by injustice, and would not justice restore it ?   What has the slave done to forfeit his libesty ?   If he should make him equal in rights to himself, or to what he is by nature, would he not eman-

cipate him ? Can he be held at all without a
violation of all the just notions of equity.
Though, therefore it may be true that this
passage only enjoins the rendering of what
was just and equal in their condition, yet it
contains a principle which would lay the axe
at the root of slavery, and would lead a conscientious Christian to the feeling that his
slaves ought to be free."

The above extract is decisive, for if it be
admitted, consequences must follow fatal to
slavery.   Let us look at it upon the assumption,that the text justifies slavery,and see what
a harmony of all kinds of contradictions it
will produce.

To obey it, a man would have to "restore
his slaves to freedom." If then the text justifies slaveholding, it justifies disobedience to
its own command. They were "deprived of
their liberty by injustice, and justice would
restore it." Then if the text justifies slaveholding. it justifies injustice.

Slaves cannot " be held at all without a violation of all just notions of equity."   Then
if the text justifies slaveholding, it justifies a
violation of all the just notions of equity."
"It contains a principle which would lay the
axe at the root of slavery." If then it justifies slavery, it lays the axe at the root of the
thing it justifies.

It " would lead a conscientious. Christian
to feel that his slaves ought to be free."   If
then it justifies slaveholding, it justifies men
in acting contrary to their concientious feelings. Such are the contradictions involved

if we, in the light of **Mr.** Barns' notes, allow
that the text justifies slaveholding.

I may at this point claim that I have disposed of another of the supposed strong texts
in support of slavery, and will dismiss it with
what has been said.

PAUL TO TIMOTHY DOES NOT JUSTIFY SLAVERY.

" Let as many servants as are under the
yoke count their own masters worthy of all
honor, that the name of God and his doctrine
be not blasphemed. And they that have believing masters, let them not despise them,
because they are brethren ; but rather do
them service, because they are faithful and
beloved,partakers of the benefit."1 Tim.vi. 1,2.

This text has been supposed by some, the
most difficult one in the New Testament, for
an anti-slavery expositor to dispose of. If,
however, the reader will keep his mind on the
real issue, the text will furnish no very hard
task. The question is, does the text prove
American slavery to be right ? I am not
bound, in this issue, to prove that slavery is
wrong; the advocate of slavery is bound to
prove that this text justifies slavery, that it
contains principles which are not only applicable to American slavery, but which, when
applied, prove it to be right. I am bound, in
a fair reply, to prove no more than that it contains no such justification of slavery. That
will not be a hard task. But I will be gener-
ous and do more than the issue demands of
me.

I. It is not sufficiently certain that the

text treats of slaves and slaveholders, so as to render it a conclusive argument in support of the rightful existence of slavery. The whole ground has been gone over in the examination of other texts, with the exception of two additional points, which this text presents, viz. that some servants were under the yoke, and some had believing masters.

If slavery is not found in one or the other of these points, it is not found in the text, all other points having been already examined.

The first question then is, does, being under the yoke, imply slavery. It certainly is not sufficiently clear that the yoke implies slavery to justify a reliance upon it to prove the fact that slavery existed.

1. The Greek word *zugon*, here rendered yoke, does not mean slavery. It literally means the yoke by which oxen, horses and mules are coupled together for draught. Hence it means anything that joins two things together. It may be used in a metaphorical sense. The use of a word in a metaphorical sense, cannot determine what the thing is to which it is applied, since the known character of the thing to which it is applied, alone can determine in what metaphorical sense the word is used. If it were first proved that the servants were slaves, it would follow that yoke, as applied to them, means slavery, but that is so far from being the case, that the application of the word yoke to them, is relied upon to prove that they were slaves, and the whole argument must fall. It is reduced to a circle, thus: They were slaves because they were under the yoke, which means slavery.

The term yoke means slavery, as applied to them, because they were slaves, Such arguments prove nothing.

2. There is no other instance in the New Testament, in which the word is used to denote anything like slavery. It is used in only six instances, In one, Rev. vi., 5, it is used with strict reference to its literal sense. It is here translated a "pair of balances," because the two parts are fastened together by the beam. In every other case it is used metaphorically. Christ uses it twice, Matt. xi. 29, 30, "Take my yoke upon you." "My yoke is easy." Here it means the moral obligations of the gospel. As though he had said, take the profession and duties of my religion upon you. There is no slavery in this, though there are obligations which bind them to Christ. The same word is found Acts xv. 10, "Why tempt ye God, to put a yoke upon the necks of the disciples." Here it means the obligations of the Mosaic law, not slavery.

The other text is Gal. v., 1, "Stand fast therefore in the liberty wherewith Christ hath made us free, and be not entangled again with the yoke of bondage." Here the yoke of bondage is the obligations of the Mosaic law. Yoke means obligation, and bondage means service. It would be just as good a translation to render it, "be not entangled again with the obligation of service."

Apply these facts to the text under consideration, and there will be no slavery in it. "As many servants as are under the yoke," understand obligation, by yoke, for it means any thing that binds or couples to-

gether, and it will be plain. " Let as many
servants as are under obligation."

But the Greek word, *hosos,* rendered " as
many as"—for these three words in the English text come from the one in Greek—is not
translated in its only admissible sense. Dr.
McKnight renders it *whatever.* " Whatever
servants." It often has this sense, but
this does not exhaust its meaning. The following are the principal senses in which the
word is used : Of size, "as great as ;" of quan-
tity, "as much as ;" of space or distance, "as
far as ;" of time, "as long as ;" of number, "as
many as ;" of sound, "as loud as." It is used
of time in six texts in the New Testament,
Matt. ix. 15 : "Can the children of the bride-
chamber mourn *as long as* the bridegroom is
with them."

Mark ii. 19. "*As long as* they have the
bridegroom with them they cannot fast."

Rom. vii. 1. " The law hath dominion over
a man *as long as* he liveth."

1 Cor. vii. 39. " The wife is bound by the
law *as long as* her husband liveth."

Gal. iv. 1. " The heir, *as long as* he is a child,
differeth nothing from a servant."

2 Peter, i. 13. " I think it meet, *as long as*
I am in this tabernacle, to stir you up."

Give the word the same sense in the text
under consideration, and it will read, "As long
as servants are under obligation let them
count their own masters worthy of all honor."
There is certainly but little slavery in the
text in this form, and it is perfectly clear that
there would never have been any in it, had
not the translators and readers first originated

slavery in their own minds, to make *zugon*
mean the yoke, that is, the bondage of chattel
slavery.

If then there is no slavery in the yoke, or in
being under the yoke was there any in the
fact that some had believing masters? Surely not, for if the unbelieving masters were
not chattel slaveholders, it cannot be pretended that the believing masters were. If the
servants of the unbelieving blaspheming masters were not slaves, it cannot be supposed
that the servants of the believing masters
were.

II. If the above argument be all thrown
aside, and it be admitted that the servants under the yoke were chattel slaves, it will not
follow that slavery is right. There is no justification of slavery in the text, upon the supposition that slavery is the thing treated of.
Let it be borne in mind that I must not now
reason upon the principles of my exposition
of the text given above, that is based upon
the assumption that there was no slavery in
the case. In admitting that slavery existed,
and that Paul treated of it, for the sake of
the argument, I must set that exposition aside
and fall back upon the pro-slavery glass.
Where then, I demand, is the proof that slavery is right, that Paul sanctioned it?

1. It is not found in the fact that Paul commanded the servants under the yoke to "count
their own masters worthy of all honor."
The only reason assigned for the command,
is "that the name of God and his doctrine be
not blasphemed."   There is no intimation
that the masters had a rightful claim upon

them, but they were wicked men, who, if their christian servants did not render to them obedience and respect, would blaspheme the name of the Christian's God and oppose Christianity. But why did not Paul command these wicked masters to emancipate their slaves, if he condemned, or did not mean to sanction slavery? The answer is plain.

(1.) He was not writing to them, but to Timothy concerning the church.

(2.) He had no power or influence over these wicked heathen masters to command them.

(3.) Such a command, concerning them, would have produced the very thing his direction concerning servants was designed to prevent. It would have been an occasion of their blaspheming the name of God and his doctrine. Such a command, issued by Paul to Timothy, concerning these wicked blaspheming masters, might have led to the destruction of the infant church in that place. It was better therefore not to meet the question by a specific rule, only so far as to instruct servants so to conduct themselves towards their masters, as to provoke their wrath and opposition as little as possible, and leave the matter to the action of the gospel which would abolish slavery as fast as men were brought under its influence.

2. No sanction of slavery is found in the directions given to those servants who had believing masters. This verse comes far short of expressing the full sense of the original. The present form of the text appears to intimate that servants were in danger of despis-

ing their masters because they were brethren, whereas the fact that they were brethren in no sense tended to produce such a result, but is a good reason for not despising them, and is so designed by the apostle. This will be made plain by rendering the Greek word, *hoti*, for ; which is now rendered *because.* " Let them not despise them *for* they are brethren." It is so translated in more than two hundred and twenty-five texts.

The word *partakers*, does not begin to express the force of the Greek word, *antilamba-nomenoi*, from which it is translated. This word is compounded of *anti*, in turn, *lambano*, to take, or receive, and hence the compound word as used by the apostle, means partakers in turn. Dr. Clarke renders it " joint partakers," but his rendering is not as strictly in accordance with the original as mine.

The word translated benifit is *euergesias*, which literally means well doing, good conduct. It occurs in but one other text, Acts iv. 9, where it is translated, "good deed done." Now let me read the verse according to these renderings.

"And they that have believing masters let them not despise them, for they are brethren, but rather do them service, because they are faithful and beloved, partakers in turn of the well doing."

This clearly makes the last clause refer to the servants, as faithful and beloved partakers in turn of the benefit of their own labor ; that is, they were paid for their service. This removes all the difficulty that critics have met with in this part of the text. Dr. McKnight affirms that benefit, cannot refer to gospel benefit or salvation, and Dr. Clarke agrees with him, but intimates that it may refer to the benefits the servants receive from their masters, but has failed to explain how.   Rev. A. Barns denies that it can refer to the fact that the master receives the benefit of the servants labor, because that can be no special motive to the servant to serve faithfully, the force of which all must feel.   He therefore construes it to mean the benefit which the gospel imparts ; the very thing which Drs. McKnight and Clarke deny.   The advantage of my translation is, it escapes both these difficulties, besides being more in accordance with the sense of the original, making the true sense to run thus : Let them not despise them, but rather let them do them service, because they, the servants, are faithful and beloved, partakers in turn of the well doing, by receiving a fair compensation for their labor.   I have no doubt this is what Paul meant, and surely it is entirely free from any direct or implied sanction of chattel slavery.

I have now shown, first, that it is very far from being clear that there is real slavery involved in any part of the text ; and secondly, that if those servants who are said to be under the yoke, were slaves, that slavery existed outside of the church, and those servants who served believing masters, were not slaves, but served voluntarily for wages received.

PAUL TO PHILEMON DOES NOT JUSTIFY SLAVERY.

This epistle of Paul to Philemon has been claimed as one of the strongest proofs of the existence of slavery in the primitive churches under apostolic sanction. As it is both brief and important I will first spread upon my page that portion which is supposed to relate to slavery, and then proceed to examine it.

Paul was a prisoner in Rome, and Philemon is suppoeed to have been an inhabitant of Colosse. Paul wrote him a letter by a person named Onesimus, in which the following words occurred concerning the bearer :

I beseech thee for my son Onesimus, whom I have begotten in my bonds ; which in time past was to thee unprofitable, but now profitable to thee and to me ; whom I have sent again : thou therefore receive him, that is my own bowels ; whom I would have retained with me, that in thy stead he might have ministered unto me in the bonds of the gospel ; but without thy mind would I do nothing ; that thy benefit should not be as it were of necessity, but willingly.

For perhaps he therefore departed for a season, that thou shouldest receive him for ever ; not now as a servant, but above a servant, a brother beloved, specially to me, but how much more unto thee, both in the flesh, and in the Lord ? If thou count me therefore a partner, receive him as myself, If he hath wronged thee, or oweth thee aught, put that on mine account ; I Paul have written it with my own hand, I will repay it : albeit I do not say to thee how thou owest unto me

even thine own self besides.   Yea, brother,
let me have joy of thee in the Lord : refresh
my bowels in the Lord.   Having confidence
in thy obedience I wrote unto thee, knowing
that thou wilt also do more than I say."

It is assured from the above record that
Philemon was a slaveholder, and that Onesimus was his slave, and that the slave, having
run away from his master, St. Paul sent him
back to the house of bondage from which he
had escaped.

It is certainly remarkable on what slight
evidence such grave conclusions are made to
rest.   There is no certain proof that there was
any chattel slavery in the case, but undeniable and unanswerable proof that Onesimus
was not a slave.

I. The evidence relied upon to prove the
main facts in support of slavery is wholly insufficient.   The points involved shall be noticed in order.

1. Onesimus was the servant of Philemon.
That he was a servant is implied, not affirmed.   It is said, "that thou shouldst receive
him forever, not now as a servant (*doulon*) but
above a servant, a brother beloved."   It is
freely admitted that these words imply that
Onesimus had been a servant, but this is no
proof that he was or had ever been a slave.
It has been proved in a preceeding argument
that the word here used, *doulos*, does not necessarily mean a slave but is used to denote
free hired laborers, ministers and public officers.   The reader is referred to the inquiry
into the meaning of this word on page 109.
Onesimus may then have been a free man in

the employ of Philemon, or he may have been bound to him, as a minor by his parents or guardians, or he may have bound himself to serve for a time, and have taken up his wages in advance, and then run away. Any of these suppositions are much more reasonable than to suppose he was a slave. The fact that he is called a servant, *doulos,* does not and cannot prove that he was a slave, for Paul declares himself to be the servant of Christ, and also the servant of the church.

2. Onesimus run away from Philemon, or left his employ improperly and without his consent. This is not affirmed, but is too clearly implied to be denied. But this does not furnish the slightest proof that he was a slave, for slaves are not the only persons that run away. It is not uncommon for indebted apprentices, and free persons laboring under contracts to depart indebted to the master or employer. Such most clearly appears to have been the case of Onesimus. That he went of in Philemon's debt is more than probable, from the expression of St. Paul, "If he hath wronged thee, or oweth thee aught, put that to mine account." The wronging spoken of must have been of a property naturel, or it could not have been changed even to Paul. A crime or moral wrong could not be changed over to Paul. It is certain therefore that Onesimus must have borrowed money of Philemon, in which case he would have owed him , or he must have taken up his wages, or received his pay in advance on a contract for service which he left without

performing, in which case he would have wronged him, besides owing him. The whole face of the epistle goes much further to prove such a departure from pecuniary obligations, than from chattel bondage.

3. Paul sent Onesimus back to Philemon, which is regarded by the advocates of slavery as proof positive, not only that he was a slave, but that it is right and a solemn duty to return all fugitive slaves to their masters. This is all an unfounded assumption. There is no proof that Paul sent him back, in the only sense in which a fugitive slave can be sent back to his master. One great fact settles this point, which is this, however clearly it may be seen that Paul sent him back, it is equally clear that Onesimus went voluntarily, of his own free will and accord. This clearly proves that there could have been no coercive servitude in the case. Though it must appear obvious upon the face of the facts, that Onesimus returned voluntarily, it may be well to glance at the proof.

(1.) The expression, "whom I have sent again," is not conclusive proof of an authoritative and coercive sending. I will save the labor of a criticism, by quoting from the Rev. A. Barns. That able writer says, "It is commonly *assumed* that his returning again was at the *instigation* of the apostle, and that this furnishes an instance of his belief that runaway slaves should be sent back to their masters. But, besides that their is no certain evidence that he ever was *a slave*, there is as little proof that he returned at the instigation of Paul, or that his return was not wholly vol-

untary on his part.   For the only expression
which the apostle uses on this subject (ver.
12), whom I have sent again—*anapempa*—
does not necessarily imply that he even *proposed* it to him, still less that he *commanded* it.
It is a word of such general import, that it
would be employed on the supposition that
Onesimus *desired* to return, and that Paul,
who had a strong wish to retain him, to aid
him in the same way that Philemon himself
would do if he were with him (comp. ver. 13,)
had, on the whole, concluded to part with
him, and to send him again, with a letter, to
his friend Philemon.   There is nothing in the
statement which forbids us to suppose that
Onesimus was himself *disposed* to return to
Philemon, and that Paul 'sent' him at his own
request."

(2.) The apostle had no means of sending
him back against his own choice.   There
were no marshals to seize and chain fugitive
slaves and carry them back to their masters.
There was no provision for paying the expen-
ses of a forcible return out the public treasury,
including the chartering of vessels and the
employment of companies of dragoons. Rome
was more than a thousand miles from Colosse,
where Philemon resided, to whom Onesimus
is supposed to have been sent, and when we
consider that there were then no steamboats,
railroads, mail lines, and expresses by which
boxed up negroes can now be sent, it must
be perfectly certain that Paul could not have
returned Onesimus against his will, without
an armed governmental express, which Rome
was never mean enough to provide for the re-

turn of fugitives from bondage. Nor can it be supposed that Paul could have secured any such arrangement, had the thing been possible in itself, for he was at the time a prisoner in bonds.

(3.) The fact that Onesimus was made the bearer of a letter setting forth Paul's wishes, and urging Philemon to receive him kindly, is irresistible proof that it was all a voluntary operation on the part of Onesimus. Despatched with a communication on a journey of more than a thousand miles, he must often have had every opportunity to have escaped. He could have stopped any where short of his journey's end, or gone in any other direction, with the most perfect safety to himself, for there could have been neither slave catcher, marshal or blood hound upon his track.

(4.) To assume that necessity impelled him to return to a chattel bondage, on the ground that he could not provide for his own wants, without a master to do it for him, is too absurd to be made the basis of an argument. He was capable of making his escape, and of finding his way to Rome, which, at that age, was more than it would now be for a man to work his way around the world. Paul declares it desirable for him to retain Onesimus to administer to him in his bonds. It must be clear therefore that in Rome he was capable of doing more than merely to provide for his own wants, he was capable of doing that, and assisting Paul in addition.

(5.) The supposition that Onesimus returned to a state of chattel bondage, as a moral duty required by the gospel, is the last and hopeless resort of the advocates of slavery. It has been shown that no other power could have accompanied, to conduct him safely to his former home against his own will. He willed himself to return, or he never would have found his way back. Will it then be said that by being converted under the labors of St. Paul, he became so thoroughly convinced that slavery was right, and that Philemon had such a right of property in him, as to render it his moral and christian duty to return to the condition of a chattel bondsman, as a means of glorifying God and saving his soul? Nothing else can be said, and to say this, is to abandon the argument, besides contradicting the universal consciousness of mankind.

It abandons the argument, because it gives up the point that Paul sent him back as a fugitive slave, against his own will. The moment it is claimed that Onesimus returned from a sense of moral obligation, the idea of coercive slavery vanishes, and the most essential element of American slavery is blotted from the record. In that case there was no slavery involved, except such as was submitted to by the slave from choice, since he had it in his power to have avoided it had he thought best so to do. If American slavery was made to rest upon the choice of the slaves, we certainly should feel much less disposed to oppose it than we now do. If the Congress of the United States will so modify the fugitive slave bill, as to secure the return of fugitives only by the use of the same means

as those by which Onesimus was returned,
there will be no more forcible rescues. There
are not wanting enough Doctors of Divinity
in the North, who claim that slavery is right.
Now let Congress enact that it shall be lawful for each Doctor of Divinity to advise each
fugitive slave to return to his master, and on
obtaining his consent, to write a letter to said
master, advising and entreating him to receive
his slave and to put the same into the hand of
the same fugitive slave.   Let Congress further enact, that each slave, having received
such letter addressed to his master, shall have
the right of returning, and that it shall not
be lawful for any abolitionist, judge, sheriff,
constable or other officer, or any other person, to prevent, hinder, obstruct or delay his
return.   Such a law would excite little opposition among anti-slavery men.

But to suppose that Onesimus went back to
chattel bondage from a sense of moral obligation, is to contradict the universal consciousness of mankind.   No man ever did believe, or can believe that it is right that he
should be held as a chattel slave.   Every
man's consciousness within himself, tells him
that he has a right to himself ; that his head
and feet, and hands, and ears, and eyes, and
tongue, and heart, and soul belong to himself, and are not, and cannot be the property
of another.   If Onesimus was converted to a
belief that he was the rightful property of another, then has the gospel lost its power, for
no such conversions take place in these times.
The most pious slaves in the south would escape from their masters, did they know how

to effect it.   The writer recently entertained
a very pious slave, a member of the Methodist
church in the south, who escaped.   So deeply
impressed was this man of devout prayer,
that he was wrongfully held, and that it was
right for him to escape, that he trusted in God
to assist and protect him in his flight.   He
said he prayed all the way as he traveled,
that God would guide him in the right way,
and turn his pursuers from his track.   And
from his narrow escapes, I was inclined to
believe that God heard his prayer.   Within
the last three months the writer has seen several fugitive slaves converted at the altar at
which he officiates, and on getting emancipated from the bondage of sin, a return to
physical chattel bondage, is the last thought
that enters their minds.   They shudder at
the thought of the cruel and polluting touch
of slavery more than before.   It is clear then
that there is no proof Onesimus was ever a
chattel slave.

II. There is much proof upon the face of
the record that no slavery was involved in
the relation that existed between Philemon
and Onesimus.

1. The simple fact that Paul so earnestly
exhorted Philemon to receive Onesimus, is
proof positive that the latter was not returning as a chattel slave, for no class of men
have to be so earnestly entreated to receive
their lost property when it is returned to
them.   Here the apostle talks, "I beseech thee
for my son Onesimus, whom I have sent
again ; thou therefore receive him, that is
mine own bowels." Verse 10, 12.   Again, in

verse 17, he says, "If thou count me therefore a partner, receive him as myself." It is worthy of remark that Paul does not plead with Philemon to abate the punishment Onesimus deserved, he does not plead to have him count a less number of lashes upon his nacked back ; nor yet does he plead with him, not to sell his son Onesimus to the slave dealers. There is not a word of all this, but he simply pleads that he will receive him, the last thing in all the world he would need to have asked at his hand, had he been a chattel slave. That slaveholders do not need to be moved by the pleadings of an apostle to induce them to receive returned fugitives, we have sufficient proof in the enactment of the fugitive slave law of 1850, in these United States, and in the forcible attempts that have been made to execute it, which have rocked the nation to its centre. These facts show that Onesimus could not have been a chattel slave, but must have sustained some relation to, or held some position or office in the family of Philemon, which was both respectable and advantageous to himself, the trust of which he had betrayed, and from which he had wrongfully departed ; hence Paul entreated Philemon to receive him back. No argument could be necessary to pursuade a slaveholder to receive back a returned slave.

2. The offer of Paul to assume the pecuniary responsibilities of Onesimus to Philemon, proves that the former was not a chattel slave. His words are, "If he hath wronged thee, or oweth thee ought, put that on mine account. I, Paul, have written it with mine own hand,

I will repay it." Verse 18, 19. The thing supposed here, is utterly impossible in the case of a chattel slave. A slave cannot owe. The assumed right of property in a man, so swallows up every right, power and interest that can attach to the party thus held as property, that he must be incapable of owing. Power and obligation must be co-ordinate, and cotemporaneous, hence, the assumption of a debt or an obligation to pay, expressed by the term, owe, implies a power to act, to accumulate, to own, and to transfer for one's self and own benefit, which cannot be true of a chattel slave, or he who is the property of another. St. Paul, therefore, by assuming that Onesimus might owe Philemon, as clearly and positively assumed that he was not his chattel slave. This one consideration is of itself sufficient to settle this controversy. There are other reasons which might be rendered in proof that Onesimus was not a slave, but I will not urge them, but pass to take another and final view of this epistle.

III. If it were admitted that Onesimus was a lawful chattel slave, when he ran away, it would be clear from the language of the epistle, that Paul did not send him back as a slave, but commanded his freedom to be given him. To contend that he was a slave, must prove fatal to the right of slavery, since Paul clearly and unequivocally ordered his emancipation upon the supposition that he was a slave.

The apostle specifies to Philemon too plainly how he was to receive Onesimus, to be misunderstood, and in such terms as to for-

ever exclude chattel slavery from the rela
tion.

1. He was to receive him "not now as a
servant, but above a servant." Suppose then
that he was a slave, and that the word here
used, *doulos*, means slave, and the whole
clause will read thus : "Perhaps he therefore
departed for a season, that thou shouldest receive him for ever ; not now as a *slave* but
above a *slave*." Is not this making an end of
all slavery in the case. It certainly is, unless
it can be proved that a man can be a slave,
and above a slave at the same time, which
strikes me as impossible, unless a man can
get above himself. Paul cannot have sent
him back as a slave, and Philemon cannot
have received him as a slave, unless a man
can be received as a slave, and not be receiv
ed as a slave at the same time ; for the words
are, "that thou shouldst receive him, not now
as a slave." Such is the fatal consequence
to slavery if it be admitted that Onesimus
was a slave, and if we, accordingly, render
the word *doulos* slave.

2. Paul instructed Philemon to receive
Onesimus as he would receive him. His words
are, "If thou count me therefore a partner,
receive him as myself." Verse 17. Here it
is plain that Philemon was exhorted to receive Onesimus as he would have received
Paul himself. Then must he have received
him as an equal, as a Christian brother, as a
fellow laborer, and if so, he could not receive
him or regard him as his slave. It is not
possible that he should receive him as a fugi
tive slave returned, and at the same time re-

ceive him as he would have received Paul.
The expression, "if thou count me a partner,"
places Onesimus on a perfect Christian level
with Philemon. Paul here places himself before Philemon as his partner, and then requires him to receive Onesimus as himself.
The Greek word *koinonos* here rendered partner, occurs ten times, in the Testament, and
is translated as follows :

It is translated partners three times, twice
besides this text. James and John are said
to have been *partners* with Peter in the fish-
ing business. Luke v. 10. Paul declares
that Titus is his *partner* and fellow laborer.
2 Cor. viii. 23.

It is rendered partaker five times. Matt.
xxiii. 30 ; 1 Cor. x. 18 ; 2 Cor. i. 7 ; 1 Peter
v. 1 ; 2 Peter i. 4.

It is translated fellowship once. 1 Cor. x.
20. Once it is rendered companions, Heb. x.
33.

In every case in which the word is used, it
implies equality in a sense which renders it
impossible to conceive of a slaveholder and
his chattel slave as partners, yet this is the
relation which Paul marked out for Philemon
and Onesimus.

3. With the above agrees the few facts
known of Onesimus. The subscription to
the epistle to the Colossians reads thus,
"Written from Rome to the Colossians, by
Tychicus and Onesimus." From this it appears that the same person was one of the
bearers of that important letter. This is
confirmed in Chap. iv. 7–9. Here both are
said to be sent by Paul. Of Onesimus it is

said, "With Onesimus a faithful and beloved
brother who is one of you." The most obvious sense is that Onesimus was a member
of the Church at Colosse. He could not have
been so when sent with the letter to Philemon. He must then, after his reconciliation
to Philemon through Paul's intervention, soon
have returned to Rome, and been sent as a
messenger to the Colossian Church. This
proves clear enough that he was not a chattel
slave, and here I rest my argument on this
epistle.

PAUL TO TITUS DOES NOT JUSTIFY SLAVERY.

"Exhort servants to be obedient unto their
own masters, and to please them well in all
things; not answering again; not purloining,
but shewing all good fidelity; that they may
adorn the doctrine of God our Saviour in
all things." Titus ii. 9, 10.

But little need be said on this text, after
what has preceded, for nearly every point has
been treated, and it appears only necessary to
remark that not a word is said which is not
applicable to more or less persons in every
community, where slavery has no existence,
and of course, it cannot prove the existence
of slavery.

It will be observed that in the ninth verse
the translators have added four words not
found in the original. They are, " exhort,"
"and," " them" and " things." Leaving these
words out, the verse reads, " Servants to be
obedient unto their own masters, to please well
in all : not answering again." This might all

be said to hired laborers as has been shown in remarks already made upon other texts.

But the language of the tenth verse clearly implies a state of things very different from slavery.

"Not purloining." This is much more applicable to a free agent with his own property interests, who has charge of another man's business and funds, than it is to a slave, who can have nothing which he can call his own, and whose crime would be established, if aught was found in his possession. The Greek word occurs in but one other place, Acts v. 1, 2, where it is found twice in the same connection, and is rendered, "keep back," and "kept back." The sense is plain ; in the connection in which it is applied to servants, it forbids the appropriating of the property of their masters to their own use, which is a crime to which free hired agents are more exposed than slaves.

The matter is made still more clear by the antithesis, "Not purloining, but showing all good fidelity." The word fidelity is not a true rendering of the original, it should be faith. Fidelity implies a simple discharge of obligations on the part of any accountable agent, but "good faith," as it ought to read, implies a mutual treaty, covenant or trust reposed. "Good faith" is kept between two parties, and implies mutually and voluntarily assumed obligations, and mutual trust reposed. That the word here used should be rendered faith, is very clear from the fact that it occurs two hundred and fifty-nine times in the New Testament, and is rendered faith in

every case except two. Acts xvii. 31, it is
rendered "assurance," and in this place, it is
rendered "fidelity." In the other 257 cases
it is translated faith. Calling it faith, the
clause should read thus: "Not purloining, but
showing all good faith." There is no proof
of slavery in this, for "good faith implies
voluntarily assumed obligations, and mutual
trust in each other. It implies the very relation that subsists between the employer and
employed, where both parties are free.

PETER DOES NOT JUSTIFY SLAVERY.

"Servants, be subject to your masters with
all fear ; not only to the good and gentle, but
also to the froward. For this is thank-wor-
thy, if a man for conscience toward God endure grief, suffering wrongfully. For what
glory is it, if, when ye be buffeted for your
faults, ye shall take it patiently ? but if, when
ye do well, and suffer for it, ye take it patiently, this is acceptable with God. For
even hereunto were ye called : because Christ
also suffered for us, leaving us an example,
that ye should follow his steps." 1 Peter ii.
18–21.

We here meet with a new word rendered
servant, not found in any of the preceding
texts. It is *oiketai*, and its first and literal
meaning is, "an inmate of one's house." It is
derived from *oikos*, a house, and hence an inmate of one's house, a household servant.
The words of the apostle apply to such servants as were employed as domestics, servants, whose business was in the house. It

does not prove that they were slaves, but
only that they served in the house, whether
bond or free.

Most of the terms have been explained in
remarks made upon other texts. The expression, "subject with fear," has been explained sufficiently, in remarks offered upon
Eph. vi. 5, where the expression "fear and
trembling" occurs.

An examination of what is peculiar to this
text, will show that it does not prove the existence of slavery, and that it does not justify
it upon the supposition that it did exist. No
directions are given to masters, and hence it
is fair to suppose the class of persons referred
to, were not members of the Church. Some
of them we know were not, for they are represented as "froward," and as inflicting
grief upon their servants, "conscience toward
God." Such persons were not Christians,
and if they held slaves, it would not prove it
to be right. But some are represented as
"good and gentle," and were not they members of the Church and Christians? There
is no proof that they were. The Greek word
agathos, good, does not mean a Christian, nor
goodness in a high moral sense. It is applied
to all kinds of nouns, and means only that
the noun is good in its kind, as "good gifts,
good tree, good things, good treasure, good
fruits, good works, good days, good ground."
In this text it qualifies masters, understood,
and good masters are not necessarily Christians, or members of the church. Nor does
the word "gentle" imply that they were
Christians. The Greek word *epieikees*, means

not only gentle, but mild, patient, moderate.
It occurs five times in the New Testament.
Once it is translated "moderation;" (Phil.
iv. 5;) once it is rendered "patient;" (2 Tim.
iii. 3;) and three times it is rendered gentle.
These three cases are Titus iii. 2, and James
iii. 17 and 1 Peter ii. 18. There is then no
proof that the masters referred to were members of the Church, but evidence that they
were not. If they were slaveholders, therefore, it is no proof that slavery is right. If
we look at the directions given to the servants, they neither prove the existence of
slavery, nor yet that it is right, if it did exist.

The only point involved in these instruc-
tions, which has not been sufficiently met, is
the fact implied that the servants were liable
to be buffeted. This word, *kolaphizo*, buffet,
more properly means to box the ears with
the hand, but may denote beating of any kind.
The fact that they were liable to be beaten
does not prove that they were slaves, for the
following reasons :

1. Beating was a common punishment inflicted for minor offenses, upon free persons
as well as upon slaves. That custom has
come down to our own times, and though it
is now nearly abolished, persons are still
punished at the whipping post for minor offenses in some of these States.

2. Christians generally were liable to be
buffeted at that time, and even the apostles
themselves were buffeted. Paul says, "Even
unto this present hour, we both hunger and
thirst. and are naked and are buffeted."

1 Cor. iv. 2.   At a time when all Christians, and especially ministers were liable to be buffeted, the fact that servants were liable to be buffeted, cannot prove that they were slaves.

3. The advice of the apostle has often been applicable, and called for, in our day, where no slavery existed.   Children and apprentices have often been buffeted in the free States of this free country, on account of their religion, not only by infidels, but by members of churches, because, their children persisted in attending the meetings of a different denomination from the one they preferred. I know a young lady who was most severely buffeted by her father for attending a meeting contrary to his orders, he being a member of another church.   I am well aquainted with a minister of the gospel, who, when a youth, was buffeted and dragged out of the house, by the hair of his head, by his own father, because he persisted in attending the meetings of a different denomination from the one the father preferred.   If such things can occur in a Christian community, it must be plain that the fact that servants were liable to be buffeted among heathen, cannot prove that they were slaves.

But allowing that they were slaves, there is not the slightest proof that slavery is right. The apostle does not endorse the buffeting in any case, not even where it is inflicted for wrong doing.   The buffeting referred to is of two kinds, that which is inflicted on account of the wrong doing of the servants, and

that which is inflicted on account of their
well doing, or without their fault.

Suppose than slaves do wrong, and are
buffeted for it, still the buffeting may be as
wrong as the conduct for which it is inflicted.
A wrong act may be wrongfully punished.
The directions of our Saviour, in relation to
smiting and resisting evil, must settle the
question that no Christian can be justified in
smiting a fellow Christian , the buffeting
therefore must be wrong though provoked
by the wrong doing of the servant. The
liability therefore of slaves to be buffeted, if
slaves they were, or the fact that they were
buffeted, cannot prove that slavery is right.
The fact that Peter cautioned them against
provoking the wrath of their wicked heathen
masters, nor yet the fact that he gave them
to understand that there would be no special
virtue in bearing the buffeting patiently, after having provoked it by bad conduct, cannot be construed into a justification of slavery nor even of the buffeting.

But they were liable to be buffeted when
they did well, and this proves that it was
wicked men and a wrong state of things of
which the apostle was treating, and no
justification for slavery, or anything else can
be inferred from the conduct of such men.
This further appears from the fact that Peter
appeals to the suffering of Christ as an example, which was wrongfully inflicted. Allowing them to have been slaves, the fact
that the apostle exhorts them not to provoke
punishment, and to bear it patiently when
they do well and yet are buffeted, appealing

to the sufferings of Christ to enforce his ex-
hortation, no more proves that they were
rightfully held as slaves, than the fact that
Christ suffered patiently, proves that his sufferings were rightfully inflicted.

I have now done, for though I have not
examined every text that some may be disposed to urge in support of slavery, I have
examined all the most important ones, so that,
if those I have examined do not prove the
rightful existence of slavery, it cannot be pretended that there are other texts that will
prove the point without them.   In the argument I have kept two points in view, namely,
the texts relied upon to support slavery, do
not prove that it ever existed in the Church,
and that, if it did exist, they do not prove it
is right.   Here I rest, and will close my argument with the words with which a more
brilliant writer commenced his.

"The spirit of slavery never seeks shelter
in the Bible of its own accord.   It grasps
the horns of the altar only in desperation—
rushing from the avenger's arm.   Like other
unclean spirits, it hateth the light, neither cometh to the light, lest its deeds
should be reproved.   Goaded to Phrenzy in
its conflicts with conscience and common
sense, denied all quarter, and hunted from
every covert, it vaults over the sacred en-
closure, and courses up and down the Bible
seeking rest and finding none.   The law of
love, glowing on every page, flashes around
it an omnipresent anguish and despair.   It
shrinks from the hated light, and howls under
the consuming touch, as demons quailed be-

fore the Son of God, and shrieked, 'Torment us not.' * * *   Its asylum is its sepulchre ; its city of refuge the city of destruction.   It flies from light into the sun ; from heat into devouring fire ; and from the voice of God into the thickest of his thunders."